AF255447

Salvific Intentionality in 1 Corinthians

Salvific Intentionality in 1 Corinthians

How Paul Cultivates the Missional Imagination of the Corinthian Community

SCOTT GOODE

WIPF & STOCK · Eugene, Oregon

SALVIFIC INTENTIONALITY IN 1 CORINTHIANS
How Paul Cultivates the Missional Imagination of the Corinthian
Community

Wipf & Stock
An Imprint of Wipf and Stock Publishers
199 W. 8th Ave., Suite 3
Eugene, OR 97401

www.wipfandstock.com

PAPERBACK ISBN: 978-1-6667-7176-3
HARDCOVER ISBN: 978-1-6667-7177-0
EBOOK ISBN: 978-1-6667-7178-7

06/30/23

In memory of the late Reverend Stephen Semenchuk
(1958 to 2019)

I am not seeking my own good but the good of many, so that they may be saved. Follow my example, as I follow the example of Christ.

—1 Cor 10:33—11:1

Contents

Preface

As a pastor *and* a student of the New Testament I believe there are few matters more important than the mission of God in the world. This book is my contribution to a long-standing debate, in Pauline and missional studies, regarding the apparent absence of a missionary mandate for the churches of the New Testament. I have chosen 1 Corinthians for two reasons. First, I find myself fascinated by both the diversity and specificity of issues within it. Perhaps uniquely among the letters of the New Testament it is more possible, and necessary, to probe at the underlying circumstances that occasion Paul's writing. Such opportunities, I will argue, provide us with unique observations of a missiology *in action*. Secondly, I felt that what was missing from the relevant literature was a sustained study of the missionary character of this letter. Such an investigation lends itself to delving beyond Paul's stated missional expectations and considering the perspective of the living community to whom the text is written—how Paul's instructions nurtured their missional imagination in the reality of first-century life in Corinth. To this end, throughout the book there is an invitation to "hear" along with those first readers how Paul's missional expectations may have been received and put into practice. How, for example, did a Christian wife convey a salvific influence upon her unbelieving husband and children? How did unbelievers come to be so readily present in the early Christian gatherings of Corinth? And how did the themes of *temple* and *glory* nurture in them a more confident missional identity?

These questions, and others like them, are important. My intention is not simply to contribute to an academic debate but to observe, through Paul's letter, the mission of God being worked out in ancient Corinth. Along the way I offer some new lines of inquiry for certain texts, the interpretations of which have for some time remained in a state of scholarly stalemate. But these technical discussions give way to what I hope is a larger goal: to offer a missiology *from below* and *in action*, in all its Corinthian complexity.

Could such an approach inform a robust missional identity for us today? As Christianity continues its sharp decline in the West, perhaps there is something we can learn from the way in which Paul addresses the Corinthian community. These early Christians were a tiny minority in a large city in which pagan idolatry was ubiquitous. Moreover, they themselves were plagued by internal strife and were hardly ready evangelists equipped to take the gospel to their city. Notwithstanding, Paul invited them to embrace a missional identity from which they were to act for the salvific interests of others in a complex socioreligious environment. As the contemporary church searches for a new self-understanding in an increasingly secular and pluralistic context, the missiological vision of this first-century letter may be just what we need. While primarily an academic contribution, I also wrote this book as a *pastor*. My hope is that practitioners will also be encouraged—both professional ministers and interested lay leaders—and that our own missiological imagination would be cultivated for our time and context.

Acknowledgments

THIS BOOK EVOLVED FROM my MTh dissertation, which I completed during 2021 and 2022. I owe an enormous debt of gratitude to my supervisor, Dr. David Neville, without whose encouragement and expertise I could not have completed either my research or the manuscript for this book. My wife, Natalie, and four children, Benjamin, Alicia, Daniel, and Nathanael, have been a constant source of support and love—they have suffered more than they should have as I juggled my pastoral responsibility and academic load. I also need to acknowledge my beloved Anglican Parish of South Wagga Wagga where I have served as the rector since 2016. The staff and people of this wonderful church, commonly referred to as South Wagga Anglican Church, or SWAC, have kindly put up with a distracted pastor and granted me some study leave throughout the course of my research. On editorial matters, I must mention Mrs. Sue Savage, Dr. Graeme McLean, and Mrs. Leanne Brown who, as my parishioners, not only endured my sermons from week to week but also applied their remarkable minds to my work—it was always better as a result. There is one further person behind this work and in whose memory I have dedicated this book: the late Reverend Stephen Semenchuk (1958 to 2019). Stephen had a profound impact upon my life and ministry. He modeled, in his personal and public life, the *salvific intentionality* which this book is about. Stephen was a true Paul, to this young (albeit less so nowadays) Timothy.

Abbreviations

BDAG	Walter Bauer, Frederick W. Danker, W. F. Arndt, and F. W. Gingrich, *A Greek-English Lexicon of the New Testament and Other Early Christian Literature*
BST	The Bible Speaks Today
BZNW	Beiheft zur Zeitschrift für die Neutestamentliche Wissenschaft
CBQ	*Catholic Biblical Quarterly*
HTR	*Harvard Theological Review*
IVP	InterVarsity Press
JBL	*Journal of Biblical Literature*
JSNT	*Journal for the Study of the New Testament*
JSNTSup	Journal for the Study of the New Testament Supplement
JTI	*Journal of Theological Interpretation*
LNTS	Library of New Testament Studies
LXX	*Septuaginta*
NICNT	The New International Commentary on the New Testament

NIGTC	The New International Greek Testament Commentary
NSBT	New Studies in Biblical Theology
NTS	*New Testament Studies*
SBL	Studies in Biblical Literature
TynBul	*Tyndale Bulletin*
WUNT	Wissenschaftliche Untersuchungen zum Neuen Testament
ZNTW	*Zeitschrift für die Neutestamentliche Wissenschaft*

Introduction

The Great Omission

The church exists primarily for the sake of those who are still outside it.

—William Temple[1]

THIS OFTEN-QUOTED STATEMENT, BELONGING to Church of England priest William Temple (who served as Archbishop of Canterbury, 1942 to 1944), expresses a popular sentiment regarding the role of the church in contemporary missionary endeavors. Yet, while there is ample evidence in the New Testament of a centrifugal apostolic missionary directive (e.g., Matt 28:16–20; Luke 24:44–49; Acts 1:1–11),[2] the same cannot be said for a corresponding mandate for the churches that those same apostles founded. That there "are fewer references to evangelistic outreach in Paul's letters than we would expect" is described by Peter O'Brien as a "riddle."[3]

THE GREAT OMISSION

This *great omission* has prompted special interest among Pauline scholars. In 1991, Paul Bowers cautioned against describing

---

1. Temple, "Church," 766.

2. For specific references to Paul's self-conscious apostolic mission see Rom 15:14–33; Gal 1:11–24; Eph 3:1–13.

3. O'Brien, *Consumed by Passion*, 138.

ecclesial missiology in terms of "active independent missionary outreach":

> We cannot speak of a definite concept unambiguously present in Paul of the church as an intended independent instrument of active mission such as Paul himself was pursuing . . . in most cases a missionary activity by the church *may* lie somewhere in the conceptual background, but either is not present in the text itself, or cannot persuasively be shown to be present there.[4]

Bowers's thesis represents a position which assigns the missionary task to distinct and gifted individuals, attributing to the church a passive *centripetal* role of attraction and partnership in evangelism. On the other side of the debate are those who argue that Paul expected the churches he founded to be independent *centrifugal* movements of active mission, themselves engaged in the task of evangelism.[5] The debate, in these terms, has become entrenched. It is made more difficult by imprecise conceptions of mission with much of the discussion depending upon subjective judgments about what constitutes either a passive or active definition of mission-commitment.

The terms of the debate were widened in 1993 when O'Brien appealed to a biblical-theological framework to answer the "riddle" of why there are so few references to evangelistic outreach in the Pauline corpus:

> When Paul refers to the fulfilment of the divine purpose, instead of focusing on what men and women are doing, he regularly highlights the *powerful advance of the gospel.* It is the divine work that the apostle frequently stresses and, although the evangelistic endeavors of Christians

---

4. Bowers, "Church and Mission in Paul," 106.

5. See the opening chapter which surveys the literature in Plummer, *Paul's Understanding of the Church's Mission*, 1–25. See Köstenberger and O'Brien, *Salvation to the Ends of the Earth*, 136. For a representative of a centripetal perspective see Bowers, "Church and Mission in Paul," 89–111. For a representative of a centrifugal perspective see Ware, "Thessalonians as a Missionary Congregation," 126–31.

are mentioned from time to time, this is not where he usually puts the emphasis.[6]

In framing his argument in this way, O'Brien anticipates aspects of the so-called missional hermeneutic movement, which would emerge more than a decade later. Such an approach not only locates Paul's thought in the *missio Dei* (the mission of God),[7] but his letters are understood to carry inherent missional assumptions. A representative of this movement is Michael Gorman, who writes, "The apostle Paul wanted the communities he addressed not merely to believe the gospel but to become the gospel, and in so doing to participate in the very life and mission of God."[8] While Gorman's idiom "become the gospel" lacks correspondence with the technical language of the New Testament,[9] it nevertheless echoes that of O'Brien's biblical-theological approach, inviting the interpreter to read Paul's letters as "witnesses to that *missio Dei* and as invitations to be part of it."[10]

Despite the emerging contribution of missional hermeneutics, there remains, in my view, an ongoing challenge in the field of New Testament studies to answer Bowers's critique—to persuasively demonstrate that the text itself presents a missionary mandate for the local church. Importantly, a contribution by John Dickson in 2003 offered a methodological adjustment, opening fresh possibilities for just such a missional reading within Pauline studies.

---

6. O'Brien, *Consumed by Passion*, 138.

7. Wright, *Mission of God*, 48–69.

8. Gorman, *Becoming the Gospel*, 2.

9. The εὐαγγελ- (euangel-) word group serves as a technical term to denote the authoritative news of Jesus Christ, on which see Köstenberger and O'Brien, *Salvation to the Ends of the Earth*, 271–74. See Dickson, "Gospel as News," 212–30.

10. Gorman, *Becoming the Gospel*, 61.

MISSION-COMMITMENT IN ACTION

In *Mission-Commitment in Ancient Judaism and in the Pauline Communities*, Dickson points out that scholars of mission typically concern themselves with the apostle's *theology of mission*—the scope thereof, as well as Paul's motivation, principles, and strategies.[11] Dickson proposes an alternative but complementary approach "from below," the focus of which rests upon "the relation of Paul's *converts* to the mission rather than that of the apostle himself."[12] By concentrating upon missional expectations, namely such "concepts and practices laid upon converts by the apostle,"[13] this methodology seeks to answer the great omission by observing an ecclesial missional vocation in action, at least in so far as Paul's expectations can be discerned.

Whereas Dickson argues for seven expressions of mission-commitment drawn from all the undisputed Pauline letters, my intention is to apply this *from below* inquiry in terms of a literary and sociorhetorical study of 1 Corinthians alone. The well-recognized occasional nature of this letter, along with the variety of circumstances it addresses, provides a unique window through which to explore the ways in which Paul seeks to shape the missional attitudes and practices of his readers. Taking this focus also offers a way of highlighting the living community behind the text—those early believers whose missional imagination was nurtured within the reality of first-century life in Corinth. By way of example, not only does knowledge of ancient Jewish and Roman marital practices illuminate Paul's meaning in 1 Cor 7:10–16, it also allows the Corinthians' implementation of his instructions to be reconstructed with some sensitivity to the social setting. To this end, throughout this book is an invitation to "hear" along with those first readers what Paul's expectations may have meant and how they could have been applied in first-century Corinth.

11. Dickson, *Mission-Commitment*, 6. A typical study in Pauline missiology can be seen in the contents page of Nissen, *New Testament and Mission*, 9–10.

12. Dickson, *Mission-Commitment*, 6.

13. Dickson, *Mission-Commitment*, 6.

MISSION AS SALVIFIC INTENTIONALITY

The word *mission* is a loaded term. In both popular discourse and missiological disciplines it typically refers to distinct efforts that agencies and professional missionaries undertake to evangelize a particular people group.[14] In a New Testament study, such a word risks anachronistic overtones in at least two ways. First, the Pauline communities of the New Testament period were mostly not sufficiently established churches from which to launch such missionary efforts. The Corinthian church was the *result* of Paul's evangelizing efforts, and thus an aspect of his ongoing apostolic oversight of the Christian community, I will argue, was to cultivate within it a missional identity *in situ*, in Corinth. Secondly, the term mission may unintentionally imply that what is primarily in view is a verbal mode of missional expression. Yet throughout 1 Corinthians Paul addresses socioethical considerations alongside, and in some cases as the basis for, verbal expressions of mission-commitment.

Given these factors, I favor Scot McKnight's sociologically sensitive description of mission:

> I define a "missionary religion" as a religion that self-consciously defines itself as a religion, one aspect of whose "self-definition" is a mission to the rest of the world, or at least a large portion of that world. This religion at the same time practices its mission through behavior that intends to evangelize nonmembers so that these nonmembers will convert to the religion.[15]

This definition highlights three important aspects for my own analysis of missiology within 1 Corinthians: self-consciousness,

---

14. See, for example, Pratt et al., *Introduction to Global Missions*, 1–15. David Bosch notes that "*missiologists* . . . have a tendency to operate with a very large brush. On the one hand, they are inclined to overlook the rich diversity of the biblical record and therefore to reduce the biblical motivation for mission to one single idea or text . . . on the other hand, they tend far too easily to read back into the Bible aspects of the missionary enterprise in which they are involved today." See Bosch, "Mission in Biblical Perspective," 532.

15. McKnight, *Light among the Gentiles*, 4–5. See the analysis by Dickson, *Mission-Commitment*, 8.

intentionality, and ethics. These concepts shed light on my central contention that Paul is deliberately cultivating a missional imagination in his readers—one in which ethics are to be understood as an integrated means of salvific agency towards others.

While the language of mission will appear throughout this book, I will privilege the notion of *salvific intentionality* to describe the "purposive, missional posture" that Paul invites the Corinthian community to adopt.[16] The advantage of this phrase, which I borrow from Michael Barram, is twofold. Not only does it offer a fresh and less encumbered way by which to refer to the type of missional intentions and actions that Paul is laying upon his readers, but in 1 Corinthians, salvific intentionality corresponds more directly to the way in which Paul connects the language of salvation with the concern that the Corinthians are to have towards each other and outsiders.

SALVATION IN 1 CORINTHIANS

The verb "to save" (σῴζω, *sōzō*) and its cognates occur nine times across 1 Corinthians and point in two distinct, yet related, directions.[17]

Vertical Salvation

The first is that which one might expect—a *vertical* description of God's decisive action in the Messiah whereby his death and resurrection inaugurates a new world order.[18] Thus, "the message of the cross" is God's power "to us who are being saved [*sōzomenois*]" (1 Cor 1:18), and it was God's pleasure "to save [*sōsai*] those who believe" (1:21; see 3:15). In 1 Cor 15:1–2 Paul reinforces that it is through the "gospel you are saved [*sōzesthe*]," after which occurs

---

16. Barram, "Pauline Mission as Salvific Intentionality," 236–37.

17. 1 Cor 1:18, 21; 3:15; 5:5; 7:16; 9:22; 10:33; 15:2.

18. Wright, *Resurrection of the Son of God*, 281.

this summary of "first importance," each clause introduced by the explanatory ὅτι (*hoti*, "that") (15:3–5):

> *that* Christ died for our sins according to the Scriptures,
>
> *that* he was buried,
>
> *that* he was raised on the third day according to the Scriptures, and
>
> *that* he appeared to Cephas, and then to the Twelve.

The twice-quoted phrase "according to the Scriptures" emphasizes two key aspects of Christology that bookend the epistle: the cosmic judgment inherent in the cross (1:18—2:16) and the victory over sin and death by Christ's resurrection (15:12–57). Salvation then is the deliverance from a current age of sin and death "in Adam" and the inauguration of a new cosmic order of resurrection "in Christ" (15:17–22; see 1:18–31).[19] The preposition ὑπέρ (*hyper*, "for," "Christ died *for* our sins," 15:3) complements Paul's conception of salvation as one which places the believer in a reconciled relationship with God "in Christ,"[20] a pithy summary of which occurs in 2 Cor 5:19: "God was reconciling the world to himself in Christ, not counting people's sins against them." This vertical dimension of salvation finds further reference in 1 Corinthians through the wide-reaching Passover theme that again frames the Messiah's death "for you": "This is my body, which is for you" (11:24; see 5:6–8; 10:1–22; 11:17–34). Throughout 1 Corinthians, salvation describes the reconciling and redemptive action of God towards humanity through the eschatological Christ event.

Horizontal Salvation

There is, however, a second and under-recognized way in which the language of salvation is employed in 1 Corinthians: *horizontally*. That is, Paul addresses his readers as responsible agents who

19. Morris, "Salvation," 166, 233.

20. ἐν Χριστῷ (*en Christō*, "in Christ"), 1 Cor 1:2, 4, 30; 3:1; 4:10, 15, 17; 15:18–20, 22, 31; 16:24.

convey salvific influence towards one another and outsiders. In 1 Cor 5:5, the immoral man is expelled by the gathering "so that his spirit may be saved [*sōthē*]." To a believer in a mixed marriage, Paul nurtures their salvific imagination as they relate to their unbelieving spouse: "Wife, for all you know, you might save [*sōseis*] your husband. Husband, for all you know, you might save [*sōseis*] your wife" (7:16, NRSV). There is also an expectation that the Corinthians imitate Paul's apostolic example: "I have become all things to all people so that by all possible means I might save [*sōzō*] some" (9:22; see 10:27–31). Moreover, during the extensive treatment of idol-food within 1 Cor 8:1—11:1, Paul develops an *accommodation ethic* intended to limit any adverse salvific impact upon one's fellow believer, "so that I will not cause them to fall" (8:13) and to cultivate a salvific imagination towards unbelievers, "so that they may be saved [*sōthōsin*]" (10:33; 10:25—11:1). Finally, in 1 Cor 14:20–25, the prophetic activity of the gathering serves as the means through which an unbeliever comes to "fall down and worship God" (14:25). Additionally, temple and glory themes, so prominent in the Old Testament prophetic conception of Israel's mediating role to the nations, are applied to the Corinthians throughout the epistle, often in connection to their relationships with outsiders (3:16–17; 6:12–20; 10:14–22; 14:25). Salvific language and concepts throughout 1 Corinthians frame a series of horizontal insider and outsider relationships in which Paul expects his readers to adopt a missional posture.

This is not to suggest that these two salvific planes can be separated. The vertical application of the gospel which Paul summarizes in 1 Cor 15:2–5 is that same message which comes by horizontal means—Paul passes on that which he received (15:1; 9:22). Likewise, the horizontal posture of salvific intention, which is to shape the prophetic activity of the gathering (14:23–24), ultimately results in a vertical experience of worship (14:25). The two axes of salvation are inextricably linked with the Christ event serving as the ultimate center of both. Yet, throughout the epistle, Paul invites the believing community to adopt a posture of horizontal salvific intentionality as they reimagine their responsibilities, callings, ethics, and gatherings, as occasions which entail vertical salvific possibilities in the lives of others. It is my contention that a description of mission as seeking the salvific welfare of both outsiders and insiders is a legitimate reading of Paul and especially of his expectations of the Corinthian community, which will be the focus of this *from below* investigation. Moreover, I intend to complement the emerging missional hermeneutic conversation by grounding the missionary consciousness and activity of the church in an explicitly New Testament study.

THE PATH AHEAD

This study will seek to demonstrate the ways in which Paul cultivates the missional imagination of his readers, expecting the Corinthians to adopt a posture of salvific intentionality within the church and towards outsiders.[21]

Chapter 1 will clarify the remedial salvific intention behind the scenario of moral formation which occurs in 1 Cor 5:1–8. In addition, an analysis of the social and theological identity of insiders and outsiders (5:9–13) will be offered as background to the salvific possibilities which appear throughout the rest of the epistle. Chapter 2 will outline Paul's invitation for the believer in a mixed marriage to imagine the salvific impact they may have upon their spouse (7:12–16). From the lengthy section 1 Cor 8:1—11:1 it will be argued (in chapter 3) that Paul employs an ethic of accommodation to govern the salvific impact within the believing community and to invite missional possibilities towards one's pagan neighbor. Particular attention will be paid to Paul's expectation of missional imitation and the way in which the origin of salvific intention finds its genesis in the Jesus tradition (10:31—11:1). Chapter 4 will

---

21. The passages which will be examined throughout this book are those closely associated with "horizontal" σῴζω (*sōzō*, "to save") language or, in the case of 1 Cor 14:20–25, conceptually linked to it. Except for 1 Cor 7:10–16 (which receives only brief mention by Dickson), the key texts in this study feature in Dickson, *Mission-Commitment*. All the key texts are also concisely summarized in Gorman, "First Corinthians and the Marks of God's *Ekklēsia*," 148–49.

explore the shared assumption, between Paul and his readers, that outsiders may indeed be present in Corinthian gatherings, and that this fact ought to govern, at least to some extent, the activities of the church for such a person's salvific welfare (14:20–25).

In each section, analysis will include the way in which Paul's readers may have "heard" and implemented the missional posture he cultivated in them. Finally, the conclusion will weave together the threads of this inquiry from below in such a way as to engage with the emerging missional hermeneutical conversation and to apply my findings to contemporary ecclesial practices. While this project is primarily a literary and rhetorical study, the investigation will draw judiciously from the sociohistorical evidence available as well as interact with the emerging discipline of social identity theory.

1

Salvific Intentionality in the (Untidy) Community

1 Cor 5:1–13

AT FIRST GLANCE IT may not be obvious why a study in salvific intentionality begins with the scenario in 1 Cor 5, which the literature traditionally associates with church discipline.[1] While the expulsion of the immoral man appears to conform to such a context, it is in 1 Cor 5:5, with Paul taking this action in partnership with the church, that we first encounter the believing community functioning as horizontal agents of salvific possibility: "Hand this man over to Satan for the destruction of the flesh, so that his spirit may be saved [*sōthē*] on the day of the Lord."[2] The aim of this chapter is to suggest a social setting that best explains the exclusion of this man, pointing to the remedial intent behind it, and then to analyze some

1. Kistemaker, "Deliver This Man to Satan," 33–45; Schreiner, "Biblical Basis for Church Discipline," §5. Note the section headings in the following: "Case for Moral Discipline" in Thiselton, *First Epistle to the Corinthians*, 382; and in Hays, *First Corinthians*, 80.

2. The language compares with that found in 1 Tim 1:20 and seems to be "quasitechnical language" indicative of formal exclusion. See Fee, *First Epistle to the Corinthians*, 208.

of the implications which Paul outlines for those inside and outside the church. These observations will help to frame three important aspects of the unfolding argument of this study: (1) the intra-community application of salvific intentionality; (2) the untidy social reality of those within the church; and (3) the way in which Paul assumes believers to be engaging with outsiders.

PRESERVING THE SOCIAL BODY

It is all too common for interpreters to claim the exclusion of the immoral man as an act of church discipline aimed at maintaining the purity of the church and its witness in the world.[3] However, there are three literary features of the text which invite caution against a simple purity reading. First, if the man and his sin are the primary threat, why does Paul not address, at any point, the man himself? Instead, it is the community who bear the brunt of Paul's critique and who are the focus of moral transformation (5:2, 6–8). Secondly, whereas most interpreters assume the metaphor of yeast (5:6–8) to be a reference to the man's immorality,[4] the context suggests that the community's boasting is in view: "Your boasting [καύχημα, *kauchēma*] is not good. Don't you know that a little yeast leavens the whole batch of dough?" (5:6). It may well be, therefore, that the misplaced Corinthian boasting (*kauchēma*), which features across 1 Cor 1–4,[5] is the antecedent of Paul's yeast metaphor.[6] Thirdly, if the immorality of the man was the funda-

3. In addition to note 1, consider the following scholars who frame it as such: Fitzmyer, *First Corinthians*, 231; Ciampa and Rosner, *First Letter to the Corinthians*, 197–98; Rice, *Paul and Patronage*, 150; Horrell, *Solidarity and Difference*, 143; Rosner, "Temple and Holiness in 1 Corinthians 5," 145; Martin, *Corinthian Body*, 169.

4. For example, see Ciampa and Rosner, *First Letter to the Corinthians*, 212–15; Hays, *First Corinthians*, 80; Martin, *Corinthian Body*, 169, 318; McNamara, "Shame the Incestuous Man," 318; Works, *Church in the Wilderness*, 152; Kistemaker, *Exposition of the First Epistle to the Corinthians*, 165.

5. The cognate verb καυχάομαι (*kauchaomai*, "to boast") appears frequently in the early chapters of 1 Corinthians (e.g., 1:29, 31; 3:21; 4:7).

6. This reading is supported by Chrysostom, "Homilies on the Epistles of

mental reason for his exclusion from the church, why did Paul not undertake this same form of church discipline against those immorally engaging with prostitutes in 1 Cor 6:12–20? Paul employs the term πορνεία (*porneia*, "immorality") frequently in 1 Cor 5–7 (see 10:6–8),[7] even while engaging in different pastoral approaches to this same vice, intending to bring the type of moral formation that corresponds to their position in Christ (6:11).[8] As a result, this study contends that the exclusion of the immoral man, in 1 Cor 5:5, must be for more complex reasons than a church purity reading can account for.

It is for such reasons that increasing numbers of interpreters frame the exclusion of the man against the backdrop of 1 Cor 1–4 as Paul's attempt to preserve the social body.[9] In this social reading, the scenario in 1 Cor 5:1–8 is understood in terms of an influential (and immoral) patron from among the factional elite (1:26–31; 11:22), whose ongoing influence in the community has resulted in a sociospiritual crisis.[10] The misplaced boasting and as-

---

Paul 15.5," 47. See Brock and Wannenwetsch, *Malady of the Christian Body*, §5; Hodge, *Commentary on 1 & 2 Corinthians*, 86.

7. The nouns πορνεία (*porneia*, "immorality") and πόρνος (*pornos*, "immoral person") between them occur nine times (1 Cor 5:1, 9, 10, 11; 6:9, 13, 18; 7:2) and the cognate verb πορνεύω (*porneuō*, "to commit immorality") on a further two occasions (6:18; 10:8). Paul also refers to πόρνη (*pornē*, "a prostitute") twice within two verses (6:15–16). Additionally, there is the vice list of 1 Cor 6:9 in which μοιχός (*moichos*, "adulterer") and the related terms μαλακός (*malakos*) and ἀρσενοκοίτης (*arsenokoitēs*) occur, both of which likely refer to aspects of homosexual practice. Moreover, conceptual ideas associated with immorality occur in 1 Cor 7:1–9 and 10:6–8.

8. While the immoral man is excluded from the community in 1 Cor 5:5, Paul adopts an approach of warning and exhortation towards those engaging with prostitutes (6:12–20), and, in 1 Cor 7:1–9, he applies the practical conjugal good of marriage as that which can assist couples against temptation.

9. I borrow this phrase from Reno, "Struggling Sages," 492–93.

10. Joshua Rice notes that by the time of the New Testament era "the patronage system had reached its cultural apex in the Roman world as the chief convention for mediating power between persons of differing status." Moreover, he suggests a "puffed-upness on behalf of teachers" such that the culprits are taking pride in Apollos over Paul. See Rice, *Paul and Patronage*, 51, 148. See deSilva, *Honor, Patronage, Kinship and Purity*, 41; Chow, *Patronage and*

sociated vices of some in the community (5:2, 6–8) represent an ongoing client-like social obligation to this man, who, despite the socioethical scandal he has created (5:1), nevertheless experiences a continuous endorsement of his status.[11] It is for this reason that Anthony Thiselton detects in Paul's expulsion formula an effect upon both the man *and* the community:

> If consigning to Satan means excluding him from the community, this spells the end of self-congratulation about their association with such a distinguished patron; while for the offender himself suffering removal from a platform of adulation to total isolation from the community would have a sobering if not devastating effect.[12]

In this reconstruction of the situation behind the text, the immorality is a compounding factor in a sociospiritual crisis, which is sufficiently threatening to the community to warrant the formal dissociation of the man by the church. Yet it is not a final judgment but a temporal one: It serves as a potential means of moral formation, for both the individual and the community, the intention of which is remedial (5:5).

THE SALVIFIC PURPOSE OF MORAL FORMATION

The purpose of the exclusion then is restorative—both for the community and for the individual. Even where an alternative interpretation of the crisis is adopted,[13] the intent of the apostle Paul is stated clearly: "So that [ἵνα, *hina*] his spirit may be saved [*sōthē*] on the day of the Lord" (1 Cor 5:5). This purpose clause

Power, 88; Barnett, *Corinthian Question*, 96–97; Thiselton, *First Epistle to the Corinthians*, 396.

11. Patronage set up a mutually beneficial yet socially obligating relationship between people and institutions that penetrated three levels of society: republican institutions (*politea*), the household community (*oikonomia*), and unofficial associations (*koinonia*). See Judge, "Social Pattern of Christian Groups," §2–4.

12. Thiselton, *First Epistle to the Corinthians*, 396.

13. For example, along the lines of the purity reading already outlined.

describes the salvific potential for the immoral man, where his present experience of exclusion is intended to achieve an ultimate inclusion by Christ. The reference to "the day of the Lord" ought not to be construed as a future reality alone but rather as a rhetorical heightening of what is at stake—the man's final state of salvation, which may be preempted in the present if the remedial intent of his exclusion proves to be effective.[14] That this purpose of his removal extends to the community as a whole is indicated through the subsequent yeast and Passover metaphors (5:6–8). The vices associated with the "old yeast" are to be replaced with the virtues of the "new unleavened batch": sincerity and truth, the result of which Paul envisions bringing salvific benefit to the whole community. Such considerations inform scholars of New Testament ethics to notice the way in which the church is not simply a place of purity but one of "moral formation." Richard Hays conveys this ecclesial purpose:

> The community demands that its members pursue holiness, while it also sustains the challenging process of character formation that is necessary for Jesus' disciples. The church must be a community whose life together provides . . . spiritual formation for everyone who comes within its circle of fellowship.[15]

The spiritual formation in 1 Cor 5 is reinforced by explicitly soteriological language, inviting the community to imagine themselves as agents of salvific good towards one another. The goal, therefore, is for those within the church to behave towards one another in a way that promotes a fellow believer's Christian status as that of washed, sanctified, and justified "in the name of the Lord Jesus Christ and by the Spirit of our God" (6:11; see

---

14. Most contemporary interpreters do not identify the restoration of the person in 2 Cor 2:5–11 with this man, on which see Guthrie, *2 Corinthians*, 130, 139–40. However, there is a long history of interpretation that does relate 1 Cor 5:1–8 and 2 Cor 2:5–11, commencing with Chrysostom, "Homilies on the Epistles of Paul to the Corinthians 4.4," 206–7. See more recently Hall, *Unity of the Corinthian Correspondence*, 227–35; and Garland, *1 Corinthians*, 174–75.

15. Hays, *Moral Vision*, 401–2.

15:24). In other words, Paul is nurturing a consciousness within the believing community in which each seeks the salvific welfare of the other. Such a goal is integral to this study and frames Paul's intra-ecclesial emphasis in his upcoming instructions concerning idol-food in 1 Cor 8–10, and his tongues/prophecy discourse in 1 Cor 14. Moreover, from within both these scenarios emerges a wider scope of the church's mission, namely, the salvific welfare of outsiders. Indeed, the occasion of the expulsion of the immoral man gives rise in 1 Cor 5:9–13 to an important clarification that Paul then makes about the nature of insider-outsider associations.

THE UNTIDY SOCIAL PROFILE OF INSIDERS AND OUTSIDERS

That the immoral man is expelled for the salvific good of himself and the church raises important questions about the social profile of the Corinthians. In the subsequent section (1 Cor 5:9–13) Paul emphasizes a distinction between *outsiders* (τοὺς ἔξω, *tous exō*) and *insiders* (τοὺς ἔσω, *tous esō*), the social and theological identity of whom will become increasingly important to the developing argument in this study. Paul's expectation that insiders dissociate themselves from a particular insider, turning him into an outsider (5:5), indicates that their social relationships, at least in this case, are far from simple. T. J. Lang recognizes the difficulty that this expulsion of the immoral man poses for insider theological identity:

> The fundamental issue animating Paul's correspondence with the Corinthian assembly is the definition of authentic Christian identity. As is the case with definitions of identity, Paul's dealings with Corinth confront questions of social and theological boundaries . . . The concern is often not simply to name insiders and outsiders but rather to distinguish between types of insiders, assorted degrees of deviancy, and fitting responses to untidy social circumstances.[16]

16. Lang, "Trouble with Insiders," 981–82.

It seems that one can "bear the name brother"[17] (τις ἀδελφὸς ὀνομαζόμενος, *tis adelphos onomazomenos*, 5:11), a "so-called brother" (REB), and yet be one with whom insiders ought not to associate (5:11). It is difficult, however, to imagine how such firm sociotheological boundaries could be consistently upheld. As noted already, despite the act of expulsion in 1 Cor 5:1–8, immorality in subsequent chapters is addressed by Paul in different ways. Despite the serious moral and theological failings of the community, so evident throughout the entire epistle,[18] exclusivist (and non-association) strategies of moral formation occur only in 1 Cor 5:1–8 and are rare across the Pauline corpus.[19] As has been argued already, a particular sociospiritual crisis best explains Paul's exclusion of the immoral man. It is also best therefore to understand the "vice lists" in 1 Cor 5:11 and 6:9–11 as a rhetorical strategy which Paul uses to remind his readers of their true "positional selves," even where their current experience might be at odds with this.[20] Thus, these warnings of non-association probably function rhetorically to reinforce Paul's exhortation for his readers to become their true "sanctified" selves (6:11)—"a new unleavened batch" (5:7). If this is correct, then implicit in Paul's rhetoric is the recognition that there are other insiders who are still to align themselves with an "authentic Christian identity." Thus, the "untidy" social nature of the Corinthian community means that intra-ecclesial salvific intentionality may also result in genuine Christian conversion for inauthentic insiders within the Corinthians' "circle of fellowship."[21]

The other important aspect of 1 Cor 5:9–13 is the way in which it assumes a significant level of social engagement between the believing community and pagan outsiders. Paul anticipates

17. My translation.

18. Consider factional pride (1:10–17; 3:1–4; 4:4–21; 5:1–8), immorality (5:1; 6:12–20; 10:8), inappropriate legal disputes (6:1–11), disregard for the "Weak" (8:1–13; 14:1–40), pagan idolatrous engagement (10:10–22), social disparity (11:17–34; 12:12–26), and unorthodox views of the resurrection (15:1–58).

19. An almost identical statement occurs only in 1 Tim 1:20.

20. López, "Does the Vice List," 59–73. See Brock and Wannenwetsch, *Malady of the Christian Body*, §5.

21. The phrase "circle of fellowship" belongs to Hays, *Moral Vision*, 401–2.

that some may misunderstand his instructions regarding non-association and think he means for them to withdraw from such relationships. To this, Paul responds emphatically, "Not at all" (5:10), treating such a conclusion as a *reductio ad absurdum*:[22] "In that case you would have to leave this world" (5:10). Despite an emphasis on group identity within Pauline communities, there are, according to Wayne Meeks, "gates in the boundaries" which Paul not only permitted but in some cases positively encouraged.[23] Dickson also highlights the way in which this text indicates the high level of social engagement that Paul considers normative between believers and outsiders:

> The combination of prefixes, συν–ανα–μίγνυμι ("mixing up together"), implies more than just "mixing" in the broad sense of mere passing "contact" with another. It means to "associate with in a close way." Thus, it probably refers to the intentional sharing of meals and social events, engaging in worship together, and so on.[24]

The evidence within 1 Corinthians supports this, suggesting that there were theological outsiders who were socially connected through household (7:12–16) and wider socioreligious networks (8:10; 10:27; 14:23–25). This expectation of what McKnight calls *integrating tendencies* reflects an ease, at least in mid-first-century Corinth, of socioreligious attitudes between Judaism (and thus early Christianity) and wider Hellenistic culture.[25] For Paul, this presented opportunities to engage outsiders in flexible ways so that his apostolic goal of saving (*sōsō*) others would be furthered

22. Meeks, *First Urban Christians*, 105.

23. Meeks, *First Urban Christians*, 105.

24. Dickson, *Mission-Commitment*, 230.

25. For integrating tendencies within Judaism towards gentiles, see McKnight, *Light among the Gentiles*, 11–18. See Tucker, "Role of Civic Identity," 73–75. Gentiles did not usually perceive Jews as a threat, and Jewish abstinence from worshiping the gods was viewed by pagans as an ethnic peculiarity. However, where the early Jesus movement became increasingly distinguishable from Judaism, it came to be viewed with increasing suspicion by the pagan population, on which see Hurtado, *Destroyer of the gods*, 15–36. See also Barnett, *Jerusalem to Illyricum*, §4.

(1 Cor 9:22). It remains the burden of this study, in subsequent chapters, to demonstrate the ways in which Paul nurtures a similar missional imagination among his converts.

CONCLUSION

This chapter has commenced a line of inquiry from below, identifying the first explicit instance of Paul's expectation that the Corinthians would engage in behavior that holds salvific potential. Despite the unenviable scenario that Paul faced, the explicit purpose of the exclusion of the man was for the salvific welfare of both the man and the community. It is this theme of intra-ecclesial salvific influence which will be a key aspect of the developing argument in subsequent chapters. However, this chapter has also identified a significant area of ambiguity: *the untidy social circumstances of those inside and outside the church.* That an influential patron-like insider would need to be excluded so that he might be saved raises the possibility that such salvific efforts within the church may not simply be matters of internal moral formation but may also be instrumental in bringing so-called brothers into an authentic Christian identity. Likewise, the assumed high level of socioreligious engagement between the believing community and the wider pagan society also indicates that the identity of outsiders is "untidy." In a strict theological sense, outsiders were unbelievers, but this did not preclude them from the reach of salvific influence due to the often-significant social association they experienced with the believing community. The chapters ahead will explore this salvific influence within mixed marriages (chapter 2), across the wider socioreligious environment of Corinth (chapter 3), and in Corinthian gatherings (chapter 4).

2

Salvific Intentionality in Mixed Marriages

1 Cor 7:10–16

DESPITE ANY INTERPRETIVE UNCERTAINTIES within 1 Cor 5:1–8, the previous chapter highlighted the principle that salvific outcomes are to govern the intra-ecclesial behavior of the Corinthians. Moreover, the possibility that salvific intentionality may extend to interactions with those outside the church was suggested as a possible reason for which Paul expected believers to maintain meaningful social engagement with the wider Corinthian society (5:9–13). It is generally accepted that approximately five years passed between Paul's founding of the church and the penning of 1 Corinthians,[1] during which time the community had grown to include a significant gentile membership.[2] Such was the socioeco-

---

1. Acts 18:1–17 associates the expulsion of the Jews from Rome by Claudius (AD 49/50) with the founding of the church in Corinth, and 1 Corinthians was likely penned around AD 55. See Barnett, *Corinthian Question*, 21–33; Thiselton, *First Epistle to the Corinthians*, 29–32.

2. The founding households who are mentioned (Acts 18:2–3; 7–8; 1 Cor 1:14, 16) number approximately four and each may have contained twelve to fifteen members. It is possible to infer from the text that at the time of writing

nomic reality of the ancient world that the ongoing association of these new converts with the household, social, and other political networks of the city were essential for their livelihoods.[3] Thus, dissociation from the "immoral, or the greedy and swindlers, or idolaters" was absurd even to Paul: "In that case you would have to leave this world" (5:10).[4] That Paul addresses mixed marriages in 1 Cor 7:12–16 is therefore unsurprising given the probability that many of the spouses of such converts, whether Jewish or gentile, may have remained in their previous religious affiliations. It is the argument of this chapter that these unbelievers (ἄπιστοι, *apistoi*) probably had, through their Christian spouses, significant ongoing contact with the believing community and that Paul nurtures, in his converts, a missional imagination to reinforce an ongoing commitment to their marriages. He does this through the conceptual language of sanctification (ἁγιάζω, *hagiazō*) which both legitimates the marriage and conveys the positive salvific influence of a believer within the relationship. The emphatic conclusion to Paul's instructions, in 1 Cor 7:16, conveys the possibility that an

---

1 Corinthians more than fifteen household groups made up the churches in Corinth. Thus, membership may have grown from eighty to around two hundred. These figures are simply possibilities and are so described in Barnett, *Corinthian Question*, 28, 225–27. Murphy-O'Connor counts fourteen male members of the Corinthian community and considers typical house sizes to postulate a base figure membership of fifty, on which see Murphy-O'Connor, *Keys to First Corinthians*, 183. However, Kloppenborg resists the counting of households and the constraints of space as the method of estimating membership. Drawing from Greco-Roman associations data, he posits membership numbers in the fifteen to thirty range. He notes, "A Christ-assembly of one hundred members would make it the largest attested cultic group in the entire Mediterranean!" See Kloppenborg, *Christ's Associations*, 110–11; see 97–123. On gentile membership, many of the matters in 1 Cor 5–10, such as immorality and idolatry, point to concerns likely related to the Greco-Roman membership of the church. Moreover, the background to head coverings (11:2–16) may be Greek and Roman conventions, and the social power dynamics that background so much of the letter likely reflect Greco-Roman status hierarchies.

3. Judge, "Social Pattern of the Christian Groups," §5, 7.

4. These descriptors, particularly that of immorality, greed, and idolatry, are typical Jewish critiques of gentile pagans, on which see Ciampa and Rosner, *First Letter to the Corinthians*, 192–94.

unbeliever may be converted through the commitment of such a spouse:

> τί γὰρ οἶδας, γύναι, εἰ τὸν ἄνδρα σώσεις; ἢ τί οἶδας, ἄνερ,
> εἰ τὴν γυναῖκα σώσεις;

> *ti gar oidas, gynai, ei ton andra sōseis? ē ti oidas, aner, ei,*
> *tēn gynaika sōseis?*

> Wife, for all you know, you might save your husband.
> Husband, for all you know, you might save your wife.
> (NRSV)

This salvific interpretation (represented here in the NRSV) is a matter of some contention. This chapter will outline the history of the interpretation of 1 Cor 7:16 and then advance an argument for salvific intentionality in mixed marriage with reference to three interrelated aspects of the literary unit 1 Cor 7:10–16: (1) the grammatical-rhetorical structure; (2) its theme of the marital good of sanctification unique to mixed marriage; and (3) the text's relation to a wider theme within the literary unit of glorifying God by reimagining one's remaining. The chapter will then conclude with an invitation to consider how the first readers would have heard Paul's instructions—both women and men in the first century, who were the living agents of this horizontal missional intention. It will be suggested that the believer would have expressed salvific influence towards their spouse in two complementary ways. First, their spouse's willingness to continue the marital arrangement would necessarily have required negotiation (7:12–13) and therefore some verbal explanation of one's faith commitment. Secondly, an *ethical apologetic*, that one's behavior is intended to attract outsiders,[5] was a means of ongoing mission-commitment within the long-term relationship.

---

5. The term ethical apologetic is borrowed from Dickson, who employs it in relation to 1 Thess 4:11–12; Phil 2:14–15; Col 4:5; 1 Tim 3:7; 6:1; and Titus 2:10, on which see Dickson, *Mission-Commitment*, ch. 9. Brian Rosner also adopts Dickson's term and applies it to the way in which 1 Cor 5 and 6:1–6 imply "that Christians ought to be aware of the fact that they live in full view of an unbelieving society and should strive to make a good impression." See Rosner, "Missionary Character of 1 Corinthians," 188–89.

THE HISTORY OF INTERPRETATION OF 1 COR 7:16

First Corinthians 7:16 is notoriously difficult to translate due to the construction τί . . . οἶδας . . . εἰ (*ti . . . oidas . . . ei*), which can be understood in two distinct ways. On the one hand, Paul could be strengthening the arm of the believer to remain committed to their marriage, in which case the phrase conveys a positive sense of salvific intentionality: "Wife, for all you know, you might save your husband. Husband, for all you know, you might save your wife" (7:16, NRSV). Alternatively, the more immediate context of the unbeliever's choice to divorce their believing spouse could be in view (7:15), in which case Paul intends to express uncertainty, dissuading unrealistic salvific hope: "How do you know, wife, whether you will save your husband? Or, how do you know, husband, whether you will save your wife?" (7:16, NIV). The history of interpretation, which favors the positive translation, has been strengthened in the modern era by Joachim Jeremias, who calls attention to the way in which the construction could express hope in comparable texts in the LXX and extant literature.[6] An example is that of LXX 2 Sam 12:22 where David reflects on his prior hopefulness, explaining to his servants that he considered the possibility that his newborn may live: ὅτι εἶπα τίς οἶδεν εἰ ἐλεήσει με κύριος καὶ ζήσεται τὸ παιδάριον (*hoti eipa tis oiden ei eleēsei me kyrios kai zēsetai to paidarion*, "I thought, 'Who knows? The Lord may be gracious to me and let the child live'"). Criticizing this position, Sakae Kubo points out that this and other examples cited by Jeremias contain subtle variations in pronouns or interrogative adverbs. Furthermore, in 1 Cor 7:16, the conjunction ἤ (*ē*) connects a second question that, if compared to LXX Ecc 2:19 (τίς οἶδεν εἰ σοφὸς ἔσται ἢ ἄφρων, *tis oiden ei sophos estai ē aphrōn*, "who knows whether that person will be wise or foolish?"), would imply an "uncertain" outcome regarding the husband: "neither pessimistic nor optimistic."[7] The meaning

---

6. Jeremias, "Die missionarische Aufgabe in der Mischehe," 259.

7. Kubo, "1 Corinthians 7:16" 539–42.

of 1 Cor 7:16, therefore, cannot be determined with reference to grammar alone, but rather requires close attention to the entire literary context of 7:10–16. In particular, the relationship between 7:16 and the previous clause of 7:15c is critical for solving the conundrum: ἐν δὲ εἰρήνῃ κέκληκεν ὑμᾶς[8] ὁ θεός (*en de eirēnē keklēken hymas ho theos*). For reasons which will subsequently be outlined, my translation accounts for the adversative δέ (*de*): "*but it is to peace we have been called by God*" (7:15c).[9]

THE GRAMMATICAL-RHETORICAL STRUCTURE OF 1 COR 7:10–11

The matter of mixed marriage falls within the literary unit of 1 Cor 7:10–16 in which Paul first addresses married believers (7:10–11) before focussing, in a lengthier section, upon those married to an unbeliever (7:12–16). Given that the instructions in each of these subunits are self-contained, there is a possibility that the grammatical-rhetorical structure of the first subunit may indicate how Paul intended to structure the second. In the first unit, commencing "To the married" (7:10), the following pattern of instruction–concession–instruction can be observed:

> *Instruction* (v. 10): To the married I give this command (not I, but the Lord): A wife must not separate from her husband.

> *Concession* (v. 11a): But if she does, she must remain unmarried or else be reconciled to her husband.

---

8. The manuscript evidence for ἡμᾶς (*hēmas*, "us") instead of ὑμᾶς (*hymas*, "you") is equally strong but does not bear upon my argument.

9. As this literary analysis is undertaken it is worth bearing in mind an insight offered by Dickson, who himself is undecided about this text. He argues that a form of "salvific imagination" is present whichever interpretation is adopted. The optimistic sense would reflect a Pauline missional commitment, whereas the pessimistic connotation would provide evidence of the prior mission-commitment of some of the Corinthians themselves. In either possibility, Dickson argues, there is a "high level of concern for the salvation of others." See Dickson, *Mission-Commitment*, 340.

Instruction (v. 11b): And a husband must not divorce his wife.

The first instruction is emphatic, grounding a marital ethic of commitment in the teaching of the Lord: "I give this command (not I, but the Lord)" (7:10). Paul probably has in mind Jesus' prohibition against divorce and his affirmation of marriage according to the creation pattern of "one flesh": "Therefore what God has joined together, let no one separate" (Mark 10:8–9; see Mark 10:1–12; Matt 19:4–9).[10] Certainly, this theological description is explicit in 1 Cor 6:16 as he condemns immorality and then endorses the situational good of conjugal relations within marriage (7:1–6). While in 1 Cor 7:10, it is the wife who is prohibited from leaving her husband, Paul will conclude the subunit by addressing the husband in the same way (7:11b). The difference in verbs may well reflect subtle mechanisms in ancient divorce conventions—to the wife: "Must not separate" (7:10) and to the husband: "Must not divorce" (7:11b).[11] The way in which Paul addresses both spouses reflects the fact that in the Roman imperial period, divorce could be enacted by either spouse, and, in fact, no cause needed to be alleged and no legal procedure was required—it was a social rather than legal process.[12] This does not mean that those first female

10. Jesus' prohibition must be viewed in the context of the contemporary rabbinic debate in which the Hillelite ruling allowed divorce for any reason. Thus, it is likely that Jesus' divorce prohibition was not absolute but rather a rejection of divorce on demand. Jesus probably assumed a range of valid reasons, grounded in the Old Testament, whereby a divorce would be justified. Therefore, the exception clause, which is the most prominent example (the other is neglect—see Exod 21:1–11), found its way into Matthew's account (Matt 19:9; 5:32; Deut 42:1). See Instone-Brewer, *Divorce and Remarriage*, §6. Some discussion concerning a Pauline privilege will occur later in this chapter.

11. Thiselton, *First Epistle to the Corinthians*, 520–25.

12. Treggiari, "Marriage and Family in Roman Society," 156–59. It should be noted, however, that Augustus (27 BC to AD 14), early in his reign, established a series of laws promoting marriage. Included in these reforms was the mandate that a husband divorce his wife and prosecute her if he suspected her of adultery, on which see Cohick, *Women in the World*, 79. The first century Jewish practice allowed for women to initiate but not enact a divorce, on which see Josephus, *Ant.* 15:259. This being said, there is some attestation of wealthy

readers of 1 Corinthians heard Paul in the same way as their male counterparts did—the ancient world was hierarchical with considerable social disparity between the genders. Literary evidence rarely attests to women initiating divorce and, where they do so, they are severely criticized.[13] In contrast, Paul displays remarkable care throughout this, and the wider section, to address females with the same level of responsibility and agency as his male readers. These observations regarding the sociohistorical setting and the way in which Paul seems to resist patriarchal assumptions will feature in later analysis within this chapter.

Nestled between these two prohibitions against divorce in 1 Cor 7:10 and 7:11b is a conditional clause describing the implication if one were to leave the marriage: "But if she does [separate], she must remain unmarried or else be reconciled to her husband" (7:11a). Strictly speaking, this is addressed to the wife, but, given the literary context, it could equally apply to the husband. This expectation of remaining unmarried, or being reconciled, represents a *retrieval ethic* through which Paul seeks to reclaim the best outcome from a less than ideal scenario.[14] However, what is pertinent for the purpose of this study is the grammatical-rhetorical pattern of Paul's argument. Beginning with an overarching instruction, he then uses a concessional clause to introduce his retrieval ethic, before returning to a substantive command that mirrors the one with which he began. This self-contained pattern of instruction–concession–instruction may be suggestive of a rhetorical structure that features also in the subsequent subunit where Paul addresses mixed marriage (7:12–16). If so, this would lend support to the final clauses of this next section (7:15c–16) being understood as a return to Paul's substantive instruction of remaining married

hellenized Jewish women enacting as well as initiating divorce, on which see Instone-Brewer, *Divorce and Remarriage*, §5.

13. Treggiari, "Marriage and Family in Roman Society," 158.

14. This description conceives of ethical deliberation taking place in a schema of creation, fall, and new creation. The noetic effects of the fall are common to all humanity, including the believer. Retrieval ethics seeks to retrieve the "most good" in a fallen world, on which see Hill, *How and Why of Love*, 132–35.

(7:12). This possibility will be examined after exploring the substance of Paul's theological reasoning in relation to the sanctifying effect of the believing spouse.

THE SANCTIFYING EFFECT IN MIXED MARRIAGES

Whereas in 1 Cor 7:10–11 Paul addresses married believers more generally, in this second subunit he has in view those in mixed marriages whose unbelieving spouses consent to an ongoing marital arrangement (7:12–16). Despite acknowledging that Jesus did not specifically address such a scenario ("To the rest I say this [I, not the Lord]," 7:12), Paul applies the previous prohibition against leaving the marriage to this mixed scenario (7:12–13). He emphasizes that his instruction is no mere matter of opinion (as in 7:25–40) but retains the force of an apostolic command, as from one who has the Spirit of God (7:40). In the previous subunit, the one-flesh tradition was the theological ground for marital ethics. However, when addressing those in mixed marriages Paul introduces an additional and unique theological argument for marital commitment: "For the unbelieving husband has been sanctified through [ἡγίασται . . . ἐν, *hēgiastai . . . en*] his wife, and the unbelieving wife has been sanctified through [ἡγίασται . . . ἐν, *hēgiastai . . . en*] her believing husband" (7:14).

This development in Paul's argument may reflect a hesitancy among the Corinthian converts regarding the legitimacy of their mixed marriages.[15] The Old Testament forbade such marriages (e.g., Ezra 9–10 and Neh 13) and the rabbinic consensus in this regard was that the "unclean defiles the clean."[16] Moreover, immediately prior to his remarks about marriage, Paul had addressed the defiling effect of sexual contact with prostitutes (1 Cor 6:15–19). That such sexual sin is εἰς τὸ ἴδιον σῶμα (*eis to idion sōma*, "against the body itself," 6:18, NRSV) is said by Thiselton to hold

---

15. Thiselton, *First Epistle to the Corinthians*, 528.

16. Bailey, *Paul through Mediterranean Eyes*, 206.

"almost limitless" possibilities of interpretation, but what is clear enough is that the body (σῶμα, *sōma*) is aligned closely with temple imagery (6:19).[17] Thus, Paul's teaching may have invited questions about personal defilement in the case of ongoing marital relations with an unbelieving spouse. This problem was most acute for the Roman wife whose social, religious, and sexual obligations were centered on her husband while he was quite free to engage in extramarital intercourse.[18] Whatever the extent of defilement concerns, Chrysostom aptly conveys Paul's rhetoric of reversal: "Her cleanness overcomes the uncleanness of her husband, just as the cleanness of a believing husband overcomes the uncleanness of his unbelieving wife."[19] Given the gender disparity in ancient marriage, it is extraordinary that Paul gives such agency to the wife—he even mentions her first in conveying this sanctifying effect (1 Cor 7:14).[20] Such mixed marriages are not simply theologically legitimate but hold sanctifying potential! Whereas bad yeast leavens the whole lump of dough (1 Cor 5:6) and joining with a prostitute was defiling (1 Cor 6:16), the union of mixed marriage is of a different order and reverses the contagion. In the words of Richard Hays, "Holiness is, as it were, contagious."[21]

What, then, does Paul envision this sanctifying effect to be? So far in 1 Corinthians, the ἅγιος (*hagios*, "sanctification") word group has been associated with temple imagery and applied to the Corinthians as those who belong to God (1:2; 3:17; 6:1–2, 19). Yet, such a realist incorporation of an unbelieving spouse into this people of God is unlikely given that their salvation in 1 Cor 7:16 is phrased in terms of a future possibility (or improbability if one translates the idiom as uncertain). More likely Paul is, in the first

17. For the range of interpretive approaches see Thiselton, *First Epistle to the Corinthians*, 471–72.

18. Although not with other married women, on which see Cohick, *Women in the World*, 70–71.

19. Chrysostom, "Homilies on the Epistles of Paul 19.4," 64.

20. The reading ἀδελφῷ (*adelphō*, "brother") has earlier textual support than ἀνδρί (*andri*, "man/husband"), which was probably adopted later to balance "wife" in the first clause. See Garland, *1 Corinthians*, 296–97.

21. Hays, *First Corinthians*, 121.

instance, affirming the legitimacy of the marital union by drawing on Jewish betrothal language—such would come naturally to Paul and be familiar, at least, to the Jewish population in Corinth. By the first century, the Old Testament term for betrothal, *erubin*, which suggested the wife as "acquired," was replaced by the term *kiddushin*, "sanctified," which conveyed that the couple were set apart for each other.[22] In an important study, Yonder Gillihan demonstrates the way in which Paul applies the legal betrothal status of this Jewish tradition to those in mixed marriages in Corinth:

> The rabbis assumed that the act of betrothal, or "sanctification," implied the licitness of the marital union. This is precisely what Paul implies in 1 Cor 7:14—the marital union is licit because the unbelieving spouse is "sanctified"—a legal status typically associated with the female spouse. Paul seems to be using the Greek equivalent of a Pharisaic-rabbinic betrothal idiom.[23]

Moreover, Paul reasons, on the basis that the Corinthians already agree, that the sanctified status (ἅγιά ἐστιν, *hagia estin*, 7:14) of any children further reinforces the legitimate standing of the marriage. The question of the status of children of mixed marriages occupied Jewish thinkers in the centuries preceding and following Paul's ministry. Gillihan notes, however, that Paul departs from the accepted rabbinic thinking of his day by ruling that the offspring do not follow the status of the inferior (non-Jewish spouse) but are sanctified, "that is, have full access to the temple constituted by the sanctified community," based on the believer (as the parent) in the marriage.[24] This premise of the children's status, which the Corinthians seem to take for granted, reinforces Paul's legitimization of these marriages in Corinth: "[The] licitness of marriage is now judged on the basis of the indissolubility of the marital bond

---

22. Instone-Brewer, *Divorce and Remarriage*, §8.

23. Gillihan, "Jewish Laws on Illicit Marriage," 718.

24. Children of forbidden sexual unions were *mamzermin*, that is, forbidden to enter the temple, on which see Gillihan, "Jewish Laws on Illicit Marriage," 729.

(by the believer) rather than on the basis of the premarital status of each spouse."[25]

For those married to unbelievers in Corinth, this language of sanctification answers any doubt as to the legitimacy of their marriage in this new community of faith. Moreover, Paul is extending such language well beyond its original context to convey a rich theological notion of spiritual influence. In Jewish betrothal ceremonies the wife could only be the passive recipient of the husband's sanctifying pledge. Yet Paul extends the application to the unbelieving husband who "has been sanctified [*hēgiastai*] through his [Christian] wife" (7:14). Making reference to Gillihan's study, Ciampa and Rosner suggest "that the Christian's prior decision to commit themselves to their spouse now entails an act of having set that spouse apart to themselves, and thus to their sphere of influence."[26] Indeed, as has been noted, the original intent behind this language was, in part, to clarify legitimacy and subsequent access to God's temple. Given the way that the believer is so closely identified with the temple (6:19), Ciampa and Rosner suggest that Paul intends to extend the meaning of spousal sanctification in terms of the natural consequences or blessings of being in a marriage to a believer.[27] The mixed marriage becomes, in the words of Hays, "a sacred environment" in which certain natural benefits of witness and influence may apply that encompass salvific potential.[28] The importance of this temple motif for the missional identity of the Corinthians will continue to be developed throughout this book.

With this theological analysis in mind, it remains to return to the disputed reading of 1 Cor 7:16 and consider how the

25. Gillihan, "Jewish Laws on Illicit Marriage," 718–19.

26. Ciampa and Rosner, *First Letter to the Corinthians*, 299. Barton argues for a further meaning of holiness language by connecting it with the theme of the Shema and God's oneness, which "instead of drawing a purity line *between* the believing spouse and unbelieving spouse . . . draws a line *around* them." See Barton, "Sanctification and Oneness," 55.

27. Ciampa and Rosner, *First Letter to the Corinthians*, 301.

28. Hays, *First Corinthians*, 122. See Thiselton, *First Epistle to the Corinthians*, 529–30; Bender, *1 Corinthians*, §7.

grammatical-rhetorical structure of Paul's argument throughout this subunit might contribute to a reading of positive salvific hope.

THE GRAMMATICAL-RHETORICAL STRUCTURE OF 1 COR 7:12–16

In a pattern similar to the instruction–concession–instruction form of 1 Cor 7:10–11, after promoting his instruction (7:12–14), an adversative introduces a concessional clause (εἰ δὲ, *ei de*, "but if") which recognizes that the unbelieving spouse may choose to leave the marriage (7:15a). Consequently, the only response available to the believer in such a case is to allow them to do so: "Let it be so." This retrieval ethic is framed differently from that which was allowed in 7:11 because in this case reconciliation (presumably) is not possible, and thus the believer is "not bound" (οὐ δεδούλωται, *ou dedoulōtai*, 7:15b). In the ancient world, legitimate divorce, whether Jewish or Roman, recognized an inherent freedom to remarry, and, as such, this concession could be read as a Pauline privilege subject to the advice that will follow from 7:17–40.[29] This brings into view the critical interpretive issues associated with 7:15c–16. Should a return to the primary instruction be expected in the remaining verses of this section? Or does 7:15c–16 constitute a continuation of the concessional clause begun in 7:15a? To assist the analysis, the specific clauses are as follows (without translation so the positions may first be considered):

> v. 15a: εἰ δὲ ὁ ἄπιστος χωρίζεται, χωριζέσθω·
>
> ei de ho apistos chōrizetai, chōrizesthō;
>
> v. 15b: οὐ δεδούλωται ὁ ἀδελφὸς ἢ ἡ ἀδελφὴ ἐν τοῖς τοιτούτοις·
>
> ou dedoulōtai ho adelphos ē hē adelphē en tois toitoutois;

29. Instone-Brewer, *Divorce and Remarriage*, §7. For an argument against this Pauline privilege reading see Fee, *First Epistle to the Corinthians*, 302–5. It should be noted, however, that Fee does not believe "that Paul *disallows* remarriage in such cases; he simply does not speak to it at all."

v. 15c: ἐν δὲ εἰρήνῃ κέκληκεν ὑμᾶς ὁ θεός.

en de eirēnē keklēken hymas ho theos.

v. 16: τί γὰρ οἶδας, γύναι, εἰ τὸν ἄνδρα σώσεις; ἢ τί οἶδας, ἄνερ, εἰ τὴν γυναῖκα σώσεις;

ti gar oidas, gynai, ei ton andra sōseis?
ē ti oidas, aner, ei tēn gynaika sōseis?

Kubo argues that it is most natural and proximate to read 1 Cor 7:15c–16 as a continuation of the concessional idea commenced in 7:15a. To do this, he proposes that Paul is likely addressing two groups: one that desires the marriage to end (7:12–14) and another that is standing in the way of their partner who wishes as much (7:15–16):

> This first group referred to in vv. 12–14 includes those who felt uncomfortable about their continued cohabitation with their unbelieving partners . . . His unbelieving marriage partner is considered unclean and he feels he cannot remain with her in this type of polluting relationship. Psychologically and logically, it would be completely inappropriate at this point to suggest the possible conversion of his partner as a reason to maintain the relationship. Uppermost in his mind is the legitimacy of the relationship. Thus Paul deals with this problem in v. 14.
>
> The second group that Paul addresses are those who, even though their unbelieving partner desires to separate, would do all in their power to keep them from doing so . . . In v. 15ab, he instructs those who wish to keep their unbelieving partners who desire separation to allow them to do so. In vv. 15c and 16, he gives his reason for this by telling them that God desires peace for them, and by showing them that their motivation for doing so (the conversion of the partner) is uncertain especially since their partners want to separate.[30]

In this reconstruction, God's peace soothes the believer's anxious response, giving them a type of psychological and theological permission to let their unbelieving partners leave if they wish to

---

30. Kubo, "1 Corinthians 7:16," 543–44.

do so. Thus, 1 Cor 7:16 is translated with a sense of uncertainty to challenge unrealistic expectations: "How do you know, wife, whether you will save your husband? Or, how do you know, husband, whether you will save your wife?" (NIV).

There are several vulnerabilities in Kubo's thesis that can be probed, the first of which is grammatical. While Kubo does not address this specifically, his argument assumes that 7:15c functions as an explanatory clause—an unlikely possibility given the adversative δέ (*de*, 7:15c). Stephen Chambers, while agreeing with Kubo's overall thesis, recognizes the force of the adversative (which he translates as "rather") by suggesting that it serves to introduce the second of two reasons that the marriage be allowed to end:

> 7:15a: Imperative: But if the unbeliever separates, *let* that person separate:
>
> 7:15b: Reason #1: A brother or sister is *not* enslaved in such circumstances;
>
> 7:15c: Reason #2: *Rather*, you have been called [to be] in peace.[31]

While this is more grammatically plausible, it still suffers from a missing explanatory conjunction in 7:15b where one would expect it to introduce the reason for the imperative of 7:15a.

There are also other vulnerabilities in Kubo's argument. First, the reconstruction of a "second group" who are attempting to stop their unbelieving partners from leaving may assume too much of ancient divorce processes. As previously indicated, there was no formal period of separation, and an intention to leave the marriage was all that was required for it to end. Secondly, Kubo under-appreciates the rhetorical force of the sanctifying influence upon not only the believer's spouse but other members of their household. Finally, this thesis requires us to imagine that Paul offers, in 1 Cor 7:15c, the pastoral comfort of God's peace before concluding in 7:16 with an implied criticism of their (misplaced) missional hopes. This hardly seems pastorally congruent.

31. Chambers, "Paul, His Converts," 97. See Conzelmann, *1 Corinthians*, 123–24.

In summary, the grammar, rhetorical structure, and marital sanctification theology, in my view, together point to my following proposal and translation:

> *Instruction* (vv. 12–14): To the rest I say (I, not the Lord): If any brother has an unbelieving wife and she agrees to live with him, he must not divorce her. And if any woman has an unbelieving husband and he agrees to live with her, she must not divorce him. For the unbelieving husband is sanctified by his wife, and the unbelieving wife is sanctified by her husband. Otherwise your children would be unclean, but now they are sanctified.

> *Concession* (v. 15a–b): But if the unbeliever separates, let them separate. A brother or sister is not bound in such cases.

> *Instruction* (reinforced) (vv. 15c–16): But it is to peace we have been called by God. Wife, for all you know, you might save your husband. Husband, for all you know, you might save your wife.

This rhetorical structure mirrors the instruction–concession–instruction pattern of the prior subunit (7:10–12) and provides the most straightforward translation of δέ (*de*, "but," 7:15c) as an adversative. Further support for this conclusion comes in the use of the perfect form of the verb καλέω (*kaleō*, "to call")[32] along with the vocabulary of εἰρήνη (*eirēnē*, "peace"), which together are suggestive not of comfort for the divorce but of encouragement for the married. Throughout 1 Cor 7 the language of calling (*kaleō*) serves as an affirmation of the personal circumstances of various believers *when* they were converted. This is not a passive or stoic acceptance of fate but a "social creativity"[33]—a reimagination of how to glorify God (6:20) in a variety of personal circumstances, further reinforced by the term *peace* (*eirēnē*), which commonly

---

32. The function of the perfect tense in ensuring prominence is noted as a possibility by Ciampa and Rosner, *First Letter to the Corinthians*, 55. They reference discussion by Campbell, *Verbal Aspect and Non-Indicative Verbs*, 28–29.

33. Tucker, "1 Corinthians," 305.

reaches for the positive value of relational harmony.[34] It is significant that Brian Brock and Bernd Wannenwetsch discern the entire force of Paul's marital theology from 1 Cor 7:1 in terms of this vision:

> We only grasp the liberating force of Paul's portrayal when we grasp that as a whole it drives towards the affirmation of 7:15b: it is to peace that God has called you . . . Paul is summoning believers to no other *telos* than the one that is given to the life of the church as a whole, that is, to live as the body of reconciliation and peace (Eph 2). Patterns of sexual intimacy among Christian couples should bear witness to and draw from the power of this reconciling community.[35]

This reading of 1 Cor 7:15c, as a return to Paul's exhortation to marital commitment, renders the disputed clause of 7:16 as a heightening of the salvific possibilities of the sanctifying effect of the believer in a mixed marriage.

SALVIFIC POTENTIAL IN MIXED MARRIAGE

While the one-flesh union undergirds all marital and sexual ethics, to those in mixed marriages Paul describes a unique sanctifying effect of the believer upon their unbelieving spouse, reinforcing not only the legitimacy of their marriage but also their salvific influence. Now, in this final clause, Paul employs salvific language, best captured by the NRSV, to heighten a sense of missional imagination for the believing spouse: "Wife, for all you know, you might save your husband. Husband, for all you know, you might save your wife" (7:16). The good of marriage, therefore, extends well beyond the safeguard it may provide against immorality (7:1–7); nor is it simply a matter of social obligation, but it holds horizontal salvific potential! The conditional nature of 1 Cor 7:16 conveys

---

34. BDAG, s.v. "εἰρήνη."

35. Brock and Wannenwetsch, *Malady of the Christian Body*, §7. See Garland, *1 Corinthians*, 292; Fitzmyer, *First Corinthians*, 297, 302; Perkins, *First Corinthians*, 110; Nash, *1 Corinthians*, 202–3; Collins, *First Corinthians*, 267.

the nuance of positive possibility which invites a reimagination of one's circumstances in terms of glorifying God by remaining in the situation in which one was called. Such remaining, ironically, answers the imperative to flee immorality (1 Cor 6:18–20) by not only safeguarding against temptation (7:5) but also serving as the agent through which salvation may come to an unbelieving spouse.

Moreover, the sometimes-difficult circumstances in which the Corinthian believers may find themselves are infused with new potential as Paul introduces the notion of divine call. The verb *to call* (*kaleō*) occurs no less than nine times (1 Cor 7:15, 17, 18, 20, 21, 22, 24) and invites a self-understanding that is defined not by one's circumstances but in reference to the providence of God to whom one belongs and to whom honor is due (1 Cor 6:19; 7:7, 29–35). Brock and Wannenwetsch note the way in which calling infuses "mundane" social identities with new theological meaning:

> The majority of Paul's references to "calling" are temporally qualified references—twice in 7:18, and repeated in 20, 22, and 24: remain in whatever condition you were called. This suggests that this passage is working with a notion of calling as a temporal interruption that reconfigures social space. "When God's call to become a Christian came," we overhear Paul say, "God also opened your eyes to the setting that is particularly yours for developing your specified calling."[36]

In just a paragraph of text, a believer in a mixed marriage has been given a theological vision to strengthen their marital commitment. Perhaps they were at first doubtful of the legitimacy of their relationship and wondered what the one-flesh union meant for their purity. Paul has sought to strengthen their commitment by outlining their sanctifying influence, the importance of their calling, and the salvific effect they may have upon their spouse. Moreover, he has deliberately juxtaposed their remaining alongside the imperative to flee immorality in 1 Cor 6:18. Hence, their calling and salvific influence emerges out of their new temple identity from which they receive their sanctifying potential: "Do

36. Brock and Wannenwetsch, *Malady of the Christian Body*, §7.

you not know that your body is a temple of the Holy Spirit . . .
you are not your own . . . therefore glorify God in your body"
(6:19–20, NRSV). The temple was not only the place in which the
glory of God resided for Israel (e.g., 2 Chr 7; Ezek 43) but was
also anticipated to be the means through which the nations would
draw alongside Israel in the universal glorifying of Yahweh (1 Chr
16:23–33; Ps 96; Isa 66).[37] The missiological implications of temple
identity assumes increasing prominence from 1 Cor 8:1 where the
motif of seeking the salvific welfare of others is developed alongside that of glorifying God. Indeed, Paul's opening salutation in
1 Cor 1:2 echoes the prophetic vision of Malachi and Haggai in
envisioning the Corinthians themselves as part of this anticipated
and eschatological gentile inclusion in the worship of God (Mal
1:11; Hag 2:7).[38] All this is further evidence that this analysis of
1 Cor 7:10–16, as nurturing a theological imagination of salvific
possibility for those in mixed marriages, is entirely in line with
Paul's wider sexual ethic and concern for God's glory.

It is this connection between ethics and glorifying God
which may also be in view in the wider literary unit, 1 Cor 5–7.
Whereas the commitment to one's unbelieving spouse constitutes
an ethical stance intended to attract them to an insider identity,
the reverse may also be true—unethical behavior may repel outsiders. Such a concern is likely evident in the previously analyzed
scenario of 1 Cor 5:1–8 in which the scandalous relationship is
framed as the sort of sexual immorality that "even pagans do
not tolerate" (5:1). That Paul is concerned for reputational damage and associated shame is evident from his emphatic remark:
"It is actually reported" (Ὅλως ἀκούεται, *holōs akouetai*, 5:1). A
similar concern may be in view in the scenario of lawsuits which
follows in 1 Cor 6:1–11. In this case Paul makes a clear distinction between the Corinthian believers as οἱ ἅγιοι (*hoi hagioi*, "the
sanctified") and οἱ ἄδικοι (*hoi adikoi*, "the unrighteous") before
whom they dare to go to court (6:1). Paul's complaint is that such
lawsuits are inappropriate and the involvement of those who have

37. Ciampa and Rosner, *First Letter to the Corinthians*, 14.

38. Ciampa and Rosner, *First Letter to the Corinthians*, 57–58.

no standing in the church is to their collective shame. Although Paul's emphasis in these two scenarios lies with the internal social integrity of the community, there remains a subtle framing of their behavior in terms of a wider gentile audience that serves as a point of scandalous comparison (5:1) and contrasting status (6:1, 4–5). These two hints of reputational damage may be suggestive of the socioethical reputation of the Corinthian community being an important consideration in Paul's mind.[39] Whereas ungodly behavior draws attention to the ecclesial community for the wrong reasons, Christlike ethics, ordered to glorify God, may serve in a way analogous to the Old Testament temple—promoting the reputation of Yahweh and drawing the nations to him. This notion will be developed throughout the rest of this book, but, in the final section of this chapter, the focus returns once more to mixed marriages and to how believers in the first century may have heard and responded to Paul's exhortations.

HEARING AS FIRST READERS

So far in this chapter, the literary, rhetorical, and theological features of the text have been analyzed to demonstrate the way in which Paul cultivates the missional imagination of believers as they relate to their unbelieving spouses. Yet, Caroline Hodge offers the further challenge of exercising our own imaginations to consider the ways in which such wives and husbands in antiquity would have heard these exhortations differently.[40] As has been indicated throughout this chapter, the social setting of the New Testament was a hierarchical and status-oriented one in which women were considered naturally inferior to men.[41] Josephus, in his defense of Judaism, explains that Scripture indicates that "[a] woman is inferior to her husband in all things. Let her, therefore, be obedient

39. Rosner, "Missionary Character of 1 Corinthians," 188–89.

40. Hodge, "Married to an Unbeliever," 4, 24.

41. Cohick, *Letter to the Ephesians*, §3.B.4. See Cohick, *Women in the World*, 67–68.

to him . . . for God has given the authority to her husband."[42] Likewise, the Roman paterfamilias held significant social and legal power over all his household, and the ideal wife is depicted as one whose submission to her husband's rule is praiseworthy.[43] In that regard, the implications of Paul's instructions for Christian-Jewish mixed marriages may have been less complex than those for Christian-pagan unions. Christianity saw itself in continuity with Judaism, but there was little in common with pagan religious belief and practice.[44] The Greek philosopher Plutarch, in his *Advice to the Bride and Groom*, presents the ideal of socioreligious marital practices within a pagan household:

> A wife ought not to have friends of her own, but use her husband's as their common stock. And the first and most important of our friends are the gods. A married woman should therefore worship and recognize the gods whom her husband holds dear, and these alone. The door must be closed to strange cults and foreign superstitions. No god takes pleasure in cults performed furtively and in secret by a woman.[45]

Given this understanding, how would such a wife in Corinth have heard Paul's instructions in 1 Cor 7:12–16? On the one hand, Paul's teaching would have been empowering. Her sexual agency was described, counterculturally, as equivalent to that of her husband (7:1–6), and she was named first as an agent of sanctification towards her spouse (7:14).[46] Yet, such ideals were unlikely to be

42. Josephus, *Ag. Ap.*, 2:201.

43. For an overview of Roman patriarchy and the power of the household paterfamilias see Treggiari, "Marriage and Family," 134–41. Plutarch's idealized marriage refers to the husband's rule over his wife who is to be praised if she submits to her husband. See Plutarch, "Advice to the Bride and Groom," 7.

44. Although as Christianity emerged as a distinct movement from Judaism, there was increasing opposition and even persecution by local authorities who sought to stamp it out, on which see Hurtado, *Destroyer of the Gods*, 34–35.

45. Plutarch, "Advice to the Bride and Groom," 7.

46. For an account of Paul's "reversal" rhetoric of ancient household norms, see Lee-Barnewell, "Turning Κεφαλή on Its Head," 599–614. See Cohick, *Ephesians*, §3.C.1.

recognized by her pagan husband, and, given the household obligations incumbent upon her, it is unclear what level of freedom she may have had to practice her Christian commitment.[47] In view of her social vulnerability, Hodge invites a consideration of

> the complicated relationships among religious loyalties, gender, and social hierarchies in the ancient world, and the realities "on the ground" for early converts. Wives who had been baptized into Christ had to negotiate this new commitment in the context of the household, where they might be vulnerable to their husbands' censure . . . Yet . . . domestic religion was multifarious, adaptable, and a part of daily life. Thus Christian practices may have mixed and mingled with traditional worship practices without much conflict. Or, a wife may have been able to conduct her practices in secret . . . The kind of historical situation implied by texts like 1 Corinthians, where Christian practices might exist along side [*sic*] many others in an ancient household, suggest that conversion to Christianity could happen in a piecemeal fashion, where individuals or groups might adopt aspects of Christianity and perhaps integrate these into their traditional religious forms. In this paradigm Christianity does not arrive fully formed, but is gradually incorporated and shaped by its adherents, influenced in part by interactions with outsiders. For a Christian wife married to an unbeliever, this piecemeal incorporation took place in the intimate and quotidian context of marriage and household.[48]

Hodge's hypothesis of a wife's "piecemeal incorporation" of her faith commitment may explain why Paul, throughout 1 Corinthians, emphasizes clear moral boundaries, particularly regarding

47. For an account of how the household responsibilities of the wife and husband functioned within the Greco-Roman patronage dynamic, see Westfall, "'This Is a Great Metaphor!,'" 561–98. Michael Green draws from literary evidence of the church fathers to describe the complexity and opportunities for evangelism in the ancient household. See Green, *Evangelism in the Early Church*, 175–76, 208–11.

48. Hodge, "Married to an Unbeliever," 24–25.

idolatry. Perhaps such wives, in Paul's view, needed to conform more properly to their authentic Christian identity, fleeing idolatry and glorifying God (1 Cor 10:19, 31). Thus, while Hodge's reconstruction may be accurate, it may be so in a way that Paul does not endorse, and this may be why he recognizes that an unbelieving spouse may not be willing to live with a believer (7:12). That divorce was a viable socioeconomic option for a woman was aided by the rise in *sine manu* marriages during this era.[49] Yet, such a scenario entailed, for the women, the risk of loss regarding any children who were, under Roman law, the legal responsibility of their father.[50] In short, the social vulnerability of wives in mixed marriages was significant, and, despite Paul's expectations, Hodge's "on the ground" account is more than plausible and may explain, in part, what was observed in chapter 1 regarding Paul's ongoing pastoral task of reinforcing in his readers a genuine Christian identity.

Whatever the exact reality, a wife's salvific intentionality was most likely expressed in terms of an ethical apologetic, similar to that which is expressed in 1 Pet 3:1 where husbands "may be won over without words by the behavior of their wives."[51] This is not to suggest that verbal explanations of Christian commitment were not also important—such is implied by the negotiated willingness to continue in the marriage (1 Cor 7:12–13). However, given a wife's social and household status, her behavior remained her main means of consistently bearing witness to the gospel.

Having considered Paul's first readers from the perspective of the wife, it remains to turn briefly to the husband in a mixed marriage. The social reality of the power of the household head, both in the Jewish family and in the Roman household structure, explains

49. *Sine manu* marriage was increasingly common from the first century and limited the power of a husband by having a woman's father (or a male relative) retain control over her. Thus, her dowry would be returned to her at her husband's death or divorce. See Cohick, *Women in the World*, 100–104.

50. Treggiari, "Marriage and Family," 158.

51. See note 5 in this chapter. David Horrell describes the Petrine exhortation to live "a good way of life" as a mode of missionary engagement, on which see Horrell, "Fear, Hope, and Doing Good," 428–29.

the consistent descriptor in the book of Acts of whole households receiving Christian baptism (Acts 11:14; 16:15;[52] 16:31; 18:8; see 1 Cor 1:16). In addition to adorning the gospel through Christian behavior, the inherent positional power of the husband within his household would have opened verbal opportunities for instruction and the modeling of explicit Christian devotion. Indeed, unbelieving wives of such marriages may have found themselves socially connected to the Christian community through their husbands. Such a possibility may explain why Paul could assume outsiders to be present in such gatherings (1 Cor 14:23–25). Yet, Paul's instructions would have invited careful reflection upon such a husband's power over his family. As noted already, the reciprocal authority and decision making envisioned within the sexual relationship (7:1–6) was a distinctly Christian perspective in an otherwise patriarchal social setting. Additionally, as the husband held more social and legal power in the relationship, Paul's explicit reference to his wife's willingness to live with him (7:12) implies an expectation that a believing husband should grant some independence of religious practice to his wife. Such a scenario is a reminder of the untidy social reality of Christian identity in this early period of Christianity.

CONCLUSION

In this chapter, close attention has been given to the grammar and rhetorical structure of Paul's argument in 1 Cor 7:10–16. These two aspects, together with a theological analysis of sanctification language, have supported the claim that Paul nurtures a missional imagination in the believing spouse within a mixed marriage. While one might expect Paul to emphasize the sanctified status of a believer, surprisingly this status is also attributed to the unbelieving spouse through the agency of their believing partner. That this refers to the legitimacy of the marriage, and even to a spiritual

52. This text names Lydia as the household owner and may be indicative of her status as a wealthy widow of high social status, with functional independence from her legal guardian. See Cohick, *Women in the World*, 187–90.

influence conveyed by the believer upon their household, and not to an ultimate salvific status, is made clear by 1 Cor 7:16, which suggests that the salvation of the unbelieving partner remains a future possibility. This possibility is how Paul intensifies his rhetoric, seeking to inspire the believer to remain committed to their marriage as a means through which they can glorify God. This close association with God's glory and the community's status as the temple draws from Old Testament tradition where the temple served not simply as the point of connection between Yahweh and his people but also as the means to reach the nations. How this salvific intentionality worked out in the concrete social reality of first-century marriage, particularly for women, was imagined in the closing section, where the behavior of such a spouse in their household was described in terms of an ethical apologetic. Yet, it is also probable that, during the marital negotiation that the text references, a wife would have explained her faith commitment verbally, and certainly the husband would have retained freedom over his household to engage in Christian instruction. In the following chapter, attention will be given to a much wider literary section, 1 Cor 8:1—11:1, to consider how salvific intentionality functioned in relation to the separatist tendency inherent in the Christian rejection of pagan idolatry.

3

Salvific Intentionality in Sacred Spaces

1 Cor 8:1—11:1

THIS STUDY OF HORIZONTAL salvific intentionality began in chapter 1 with the possibility that significant levels of insider-outsider social engagement were assumed by Paul, in part, because he wanted the Corinthians to adopt a deliberate missional posture towards others. In chapter 2, mixed marriage was seen to be infused with salvific potential through the theological vision of the sanctifying influence of the believer upon her or his spouse and household. However, such integrating tendencies require balancing with what McKnight calls *resistance tendencies*. By this he means those aspects of the wider socioreligious culture that the Christian community was expected to object to or even to separate from.[1] One such example already cited is that of immorality. While the Corinthians were to maintain an integrating social association with immoral outsiders, such a vice was at odds with their own authentic Christian identity and thus was a behavior which believing insiders were to reject (1 Cor 5:1–13; see 6:9–20).

---

1. McKnight, *Light among the Gentiles*, 11–29.

While an avoidance of immorality was Paul's feature concern in 1 Cor 5–7, from 1 Cor 8:1 the "twin" gentile vice of idolatry comes into sharp focus.[2] Just as the decisive action of the community against the immoral insider is for the salvific welfare of all (1 Cor 5:1–8), so one's response to idolatry entails possibilities of salvific influence. Negatively, temple dining may encourage the Weak to eat idol-food and consequently to experience salvific ruin (8:10–13; see 10:1–22). Positively, Paul expects the Corinthians to imitate his example of seeking the salvific good of others:

> 9:22b I have become all things to all people so that by all possible means I might save [σώσω, *sōsō*] some.
>
> 11:1 Follow my example, as I follow the example of Christ.

In the former negative scenario of temple dining the context is intra-ecclesial, and Paul commends an accommodation ethic where those with knowledge concede to the Weak (8:10–13; see 10:1–22). In the latter imitation context (11:1; see 9:22b), Paul develops a wider field of vision that includes the outsider. The order of the argument in this chapter will be: (1) to outline the possible sacred spaces that lie behind 1 Cor 8 and 10; (2) to undertake a literary and rhetorical analysis of pertinent texts within the literary unit; and (3) to explore the extent to which Paul expected his readers to imitate his own mission and, by extension therefore, the mission of Christ.

SACRED SPACE IN CORINTH

The literary unit 1 Cor 8:1—11:1 commences with the customary περὶ δὲ (*peri de*, "now about") indicating that Paul is responding to prior correspondence about a situation familiar to both himself and his readers. This explains the frustrating brevity of detail regarding the social situation and why the task of reconstruction

---

2. It is widely recognized that Jewish and Christian thinking identified sexual immorality and idolatry as the twin vices of the gentiles, on which see Ciampa and Rosner, *First Letter to the Corinthians*, 21.

is so vexed. Paul's description τὰ εἰδωλόθυτα (*ta eidōlothyta*, "food sacrificed to idols," 1 Cor 8:1; see 8:4, 7, 10; 10:19, hereafter "idol-food") is likely a pejorative Jewish term describing food, particularly meat, which was associated with the cultic activities of the pagan temples.[3] Related references, which occur throughout the literary unit, include an "idol's temple" (εἰδωλεῖον, *eidōleion*, 8:10), an "idol" itself (εἴδωλον, *eidōlon*, 10:19), "idolaters" (εἰδωλολάτρης, *eidōlolatrēs*, 10:7; see 6:9), and another non-polemical rendering of "offered in sacrifice" (ἱερόθυτος, *hierothytos*, 10:28). This wide cluster of pagan-related worship terminology, along with Paul's contrasting monotheistic vision of worship (8:4–6; 10:1–22, 26, 31—11:1), indicates the importance of reading this section against the background of what Michael Suh refers to as *sacred space*.[4]

The term εἰδωλόθυτος (*eidōlothytos*, "idol-food") points to the importance of food to facilitate the engagement of a worshiper with their god. The associated activities of eating, reclining, and drinking feature in this literary unit (8:7–8, 10, 13; 9:13; 10:3–4, 14–22, 25–31) and are attested to in the available literary and portraiture evidence from the Greek and Roman periods. Suh explains that, according to Greco-Roman worship, the god was not simply the recipient of sacrifice but functioned as the "host" of the ritual in which "the god joins them in the feast when they gather together":[5]

> Ancient visitors of sanctuaries were active participants in the events that took place within, and they expected to encounter an active power . . . One of the most important rituals for engagement with the gods was participation in various meals, which above all included the act of sacrifices to the gods and the subsequent partaking of sacred portions.[6]

---

3. Smith, *From Symposium to Eucharist*, §7. For the occurrence of this term in the Apocrypha and New Testament see 4 Macc 5:2; Acts 15:29; 21:25; 1 Cor 8:1, 4, 7, 10; 10:19; Rev 2:14, 20. The equivalent gentile term ἱερόθυτόν (*hierothyton*, "offered in sacrifice") occurs in 1 Cor 10:28 and will be discussed later in this chapter.

4. Suh, *Power and Peril*, §3.

5. Suh, *Power and Peril*, §3.2.2–3.2.3.

6. Suh, *Power and Peril*, §3.2.3.

It is probable that this conception of pagan sacred space lies behind Paul's prohibition against idolatry in 1 Cor 10:1–22. The language of "participation" (κοινωνία, *koinōnia*, 10:16; μετέχω, *metechō*, "to share," 10:17, 21, 30; κοινωνός, *koinōnos*, 10:18, 20) provides a theological basis for why those who so engage in the Lord's Supper cannot also be associated with the sacrificial space of idols. Ultimately, the reader discovers that the origin of idolatry is demonic (10:20–21)—it is no place for those who share in the Lord's table, who glorify God, and who constitute a new sacred space of belonging to the Lord (10:21; see 3:16; 6:19–20; 10:31; 14:25). While Paul's prohibition against such cultic pagan activity in 1 Cor 10:1–22 is widely recognized, no such consensus exists regarding the sociohistorical setting of "temple dining" in 1 Cor 8, nor how either of these "scenes" relate to the marketplace and host-and-guest scenario of 1 Cor 10:23–30.

As far as the temple is concerned in 1 Cor 8 and 10, Wendell Willis, Jerome Murphy-O'Connor, and Dickson are among those who propose two different settings in which idol-food would have been consumed—"a full cultic feast" (as described in 10:14–22) and "merely dining in an idol's temple" (8:10).[7] The former sought the participation of the gods while the latter was a social context in which the pagan deity functioned as a mere "observer."[8] The argument rests, in part, upon literary evidence from the period which suggests that some feasts took place that were not primarily cultic but rather "essentially *social* occasions."[9] Moreover, archeological evidence indicates separate recreational and dining areas, which, although connected to the sacred precinct, had their own cooking facilities that may even have enabled private functions to cater for themselves.[10] For some, this evidence supports a reading of 1 Cor

---

7. Willis, "Paul's Instructions to the Corinthian Church," 91–95; Murphy-O'Connor, *Keys to First Corinthians*, 114–28; Dickson, *Mission-Commitment*, 232–33. See Kistemaker, *Exposition*, 273–74; Collins, *First Corinthians*, 304; Bailey, *Paul through Mediterranean Eyes*, 282.

8. For a distinction between the deity as guest, host, or miraculously present in the food, see Smith, *From Symposium to Eucharist*, §4.

9. Dickson, *Mission-Commitment*, 233.

10. Murphy-O'Connor, *St. Paul's Corinth*, 186–91. For an overview of the

8 as describing such social dining as a matter of individual conscience, and Dickson even raises the possibility that such "public restaurants" may have been the venue referred to in 1 Cor 10:27.[11]

On the other hand, Peter Gooch's analysis of the archeological evidence is more circumspect than that proposed by Willis. Gooch argues that such dining rooms "stood in an ambiguous relationship" to their respective cults and that "it would be no simple matter" for those of the day "to determine whether food served in these dining rooms was or was not idol-food."[12] Suh's reading of the literary evidence leads him to take an unequivocal view in relation to ancient temple dining, explaining that "visits to temples were never benign events."[13] This view is supported by Smith who observes that although the design of temple dining facilities was identical to those in public and private secular architecture, their incorporation into the *temenos*, or temple precinct, designated them within the sacred area and thus heightened the religious significance of any such meals.[14] Moreover, even if it was possible for some of these facilities to be "self-catered," it is not obvious that such a scenario is that which Paul references in 1 Cor 8:10. Furthermore, any such sacred association, even low-level, needs to be assessed against evidence of Jewish practices in the first century. The normative practice of abstinence from idol-food was continued in the early Christian community and was one of the few such "sensitivities" also obligated for gentile converts (Acts 15:29; 21:25). In an important contribution, Alex Cheung reviews the extensive Jewish (and less so gentile) literature of the era, noting that "food was a significant boundary marker of Jewish

---

current state of archeological evidence regarding the extent and association of sacred cults in Roman Corinth, see Bookidis, "Religion in Corinth," 141–64. See Bookidis, "Ritual Dining at Corinth," 45–61.

11. Dickson, *Mission-Commitment*, 235, 242–43.

12. Gooch, *Dangerous Food*, 26.

13. Suh, *Power and Peril*, §1.2. See Perkins, *First Corinthians*, 116–17; Nash, *1 Corinthians*, 236–44; Garland, *1 Corinthians*, 347–62; Fee, *First Epistle to the Corinthians*, 357–64; Witherington, *Conflict and Community*, 186–87; Fotopoulos, "Arguments Concerning Food," 611.

14. Smith, *From Symposium to Eucharist*, §4.

identity and that idol food was strictly forbidden among most Jews."[15] Such findings do not prove that such "social" dining did not occur, but they do suggest the improbability that devout Jewish Christians were customarily eating in dining precincts associated with pagan deities. On the balance of probabilities, Paul's own practice, and therefore what he expected of his converts (including gentile Christians), was complete avoidance of such sacred spaces. Ultimately, however, any firmer conclusions must find a basis in the literary and rhetorical features of 1 Cor 8–10.

As this analysis is undertaken, it is important to understand the implications of each social setting for this study. If Paul does allow his readers, in principle, to attend social dining occasions in temples, this by no means undermines the argument that the salvific welfare of the Weak trumps the freedom that those with knowledge consider themselves to have. If, however, as will be argued, the one sacred activity is in view throughout both 1 Cor 8 and 10:14–22, then Paul chose not to forbid such idolatry upfront, but instead first emphasized the salvific welfare of others in the community. Thus, as Gordon Fee puts it,

> Food as a matter of indifference is true about *what* one
> eats; it is not true about *where* . . . because of what it can
> do to a brother . . . Going to the temples is wrong twice:
> it is not acting in love and (later) it is fellowship in the
> demonic.[16]

What, then, does Paul gain by the inclusion of 1 Cor 8–9? Why not simply get straight to the point of forbidding what is idolatrous? The answer lies in Paul's moral vision of the Christian community—it is a place where the eternal reality of love builds each other up in the present (8:1; 13:8). Prior to pointing out the vertical danger of idolatrous participation (10:1–22), Paul first seeks to nurture an intra-ecclesial salvific concern that ought to so govern their ethics that such a prohibition would be redundant.

---

15. Cheung, *Idol Food in Corinth*, 29. See also idolatry as a resistance tendency in McKnight, *Light among the Gentiles*, 23–24.

16. Fee, "εἰδωλόθυτα Once Again," 191.

This interpretation will now be advanced through close attention to the literary and rhetorical features of the text, after which 1 Cor 10:23—11:1 will be explained as an extension of this accommodation ethic to outsiders.

SALVIFIC PERIL IN 1 COR 8 AND 10

Despite the difficulties of reconstructing the social setting behind 1 Cor 8, Paul's concern for the salvific welfare of the Weak (οἱ ἀσθενεῖς, *hoi astheneis*) is clear enough. By dining in an idol's temple (1 Cor 8:10), those with knowledge (γνῶσις, *gnōsis*) may encourage the Weak to eat idol-food and thus experience defilement (8:7, 10). Paul describes the behavior of the Knowledgeable as a sin (8:12) against the Weak whose salvation is imperiled: "So this weak brother or sister, for whom Christ died, is destroyed by your knowledge" (8:11; see 8:13). Paul is instructing the Knowledgeable to adopt an accommodation ethic in which, out of love, they forego their "right" (ἐξουσία, *exousia*, 8:9) in order to serve the salvific welfare of their fellow believers. The critical interpretive issue concerns whether the Knowledgeable have a *genuine* right, with Paul merely curbing their temple dining as a situational concession to the Weak, or whether such meals are always synonymous with sitting at the "table of demons" (1 Cor 10:21).

The first reading is the traditional one and reconstructs the scenario as an internal squabble similar to that between the Strong and the Weak in Rom 14. David Horrell writes, "As in Rom 14:23, whether a practice is ethically legitimate or not can depend, it seems, on the stance of the actor: 'Everything that is not from faith is sin.' The danger, as Paul perceives it, is that the weak will be led to destruction by the boldness of the strong."[17] Thus, in 1 Cor 8, Paul is objecting to the consumption of idol-food not because of any inherent religious danger but because it violates the conscience

17. Horrell, *Making of Christian Morality*, 124. Dickson does not use the terms Strong and Weak but does consider 1 Cor 8 in terms of this traditional view; see Dickson, *Mission-Commitment*, 237–39. See Still, "Paul's Aims Regarding εἰδωλόθυτα," 341; Conzelmann, *1 Corinthians*, 137.

of those who do not (yet) feel genuine freedom to eat such food. Murphy-O'Connor considers Paul's use of the adjective *weak* as one that is morally loaded: "The Weak, therefore, are those who up to now have been accustomed to idols . . . It is not, therefore, a good thing in itself. It is part of the baggage of one's past which should have been left behind at conversion."[18] The Strong, having the theological high ground in their knowledge that monotheism precluded the reality of so-called gods (1 Cor 8:4–6) and that idol-food was "morally neutral," brought that pressure to bear upon the Weak who ceded to it by eating.[19] The resultant "pangs of conscience" contributed towards an internal and serious feud in which the Weak angrily blamed the Strong and the Strong abandoned any genuine concern for the Weak, resorting instead to self-defense.[20] This traditional view, or a variation of it, argues that the scenario of social temple dining in 1 Cor 8 is distinct from that of cultic engagement described in 1 Cor 10:14–22, and it draws credence from the possibilities which have emerged from the literary and archeological evidence referred to earlier.

There are, however, significant challenges to this reading. First, unlike in Rom 14 in which Paul counsels mutual acceptance on disputable matters, the rhetoric in 1 Cor 8 is of a different order. The Knowledgeable are described as *sinning*—against fellow believers and thus against Christ himself (8:12). And the effect on the Weak is described in terms of salvific destruction (ἀπόλλυμι, *apollymi*, 8:11) and stumbling (σκανδαλίζω, *skandalizō*, 8:13).[21] If this scenario is a

18. Murphy-O'Connor, *Keys to First Corinthians*, 94.

19. Murphy-O'Connor, *Keys to First Corinthians*, 90.

20. Murphy-O'Connor, *Keys to First Corinthians*, 97.

21. For a summary of the scholarly discussion about the relationship between Rom 14 and 1 Cor 8 see Garland, *1 Corinthians*, 358–60. My developing argument rejects the "traditional" reading of 1 Cor 8 as analogous to the later Romans text. Although similar terminology does appear in Rom 14:15–21, the right to one's practice is a genuine freedom before God (Rom 14:22), and Paul's overall rhetoric is about *refraining* from salvific harm and towards the mutual acceptance of one another (Rom 14:1–12). This is not the case in 1 Cor 8, where Paul has in view active salvific harm and where he sarcastically employs the term *right* (authority) and where there is no provision for "temple dining in faith." Yes, they can eat food with a sacred origin (1 Cor 10:25) but not food

mere matter of conscience analogous to Rom 14, such consequences are, according to Judith Gundry Volf, "unduly severe."[22] She asks, "Can it really be that Paul warns against eternal destruction for an act contrary to an *overscrupulous, misguided* Christian conscience, an act in and of itself *permissible* for Christians?"[23] Her answer, in the end, is to interpret the salvific ruin to be partial rather than absolute and the notion of stumbling as "an occasion for sin [which] has been set up."[24] This is unconvincing in a text whose rhetoric, unlike that of Rom 14, is absolute in its criticism of the Knowledgeable. Paul concludes this section by inserting himself into the discourse: "Therefore, if what I eat causes my brother or sister to fall into sin, I will never eat meat again, so that I will not cause them to fall" (1 Cor 8:13). For some, this reference to meat, and not temple dining, reinforces that 1 Cor 8 is about a disputable rather than a prohibited matter.[25] This, however, fails to recognize that Paul is exaggerating for rhetorical purposes, to reinforce the seriousness of what he has just said—that the ruining of the Weak *is* a sin of such magnitude because it is for them that Christ died (8:11). While the theological implications of this rhetoric require serious reflection,[26] it is equally important to appreciate Paul's willingness to write not as a systematician but as a pastor who is quite willing to frame human agency in salvation in such terms from below.[27]

Secondly, the traditional reading that aligns Paul's theological position with that of the Knowledgeable is overly simplistic. Those with knowledge (*gnōsis*) are those who are not only exploiting the vulnerable but are also misguided in any freedom they think

---

with a sacrificial purpose, in temples or in private homes (8:1–13; 10:28).

22. Gundry Volf, *Paul and Perseverance*, 86.

23. Gundry Volf, *Paul and Perseverance*, 86.

24. Gundry Volf, *Paul and Perseverance*, 94–95.

25. Murphy-O'Connor, *Keys to First Corinthians*, 119–20.

26. Note Gundry Volf's comments already mentioned and her concern to "preserve" a theological doctrine of "Paul and perseverance," on which see *Paul and Perseverance*, 86–95.

27. Another example is in 1 Cor 15:2 where salvation depends on holding firmly to the gospel.

they have in dining in an idol's temple (8:10).[28] Paul is quoting their slogans regarding the nonexistence of idols (8:4) and the irrelevance of food (8:8), only to refute them in 1 Cor 8:7 (ἀλλά, *alla*, "but") and 8:9 (δέ, *de*, "however") respectively (see 10:19–20, 23). It turns out that their slogans, in the words of Thiselton, are a mere "half-truth,"[29] and Paul redirects their line of reasoning to a consequentialist ethic in which the defiling and stumbling effect on the Weak is the primary consideration (8:7, 9). While the traditional view renders συνείδησις (*syneidēsis*, 8:7, 10, 12) as an inward moral faculty and conscientiousness, the history of interpretation favors consciousness or self-awareness.[30] Indeed, in this context, the adjective ἀσθενής (*asthenēs*, "weak") modifies consciousness (8:7, 10) and functions as a noun referring to the whole person (8:9). It likely refers not to an objective descriptor that Paul is reinforcing but rather to the false perception of those who consider themselves wise (1:25, 27; 4:10; 12:22).[31] The Knowledgeable who think that "an idol is nothing" disregard those whose self-awareness is, according to them, insufficient or weak (8:4–7). The Knowledgeable think they have the right to dine in temples, but it turns out to be only in their own minds, for Christ, and Paul who follows him, are characterized not by rights but by servanthood (9:19–23; 11:1). In fact, Paul will soon gladly identify himself with the Weak in 1 Cor 9:22 and has already outlined that the so-called foolishness/weakness of God is stronger than human wisdom/strength (1:25).

---

28. An (arguably complementary) explanation of the social situation behind the two groups is advanced by Gerd Theissen, who identifies the conflict in terms of the rich and poor, the former of which would have had access to meat and the elite networks of Corinth. See Theissen, "Social Conflicts in the Corinthian Community," 371–91. For a rebuttal see Tite, "Roman Diet and Meat Consumption," 185–222. However, I cannot agree with Theissen that Paul seeks a compromise that upholds both the wishes of the Weak and Strong: "love-patriarchalism," in Theissen, *Social Setting*, 121–43.

29. Thiselton, *First Epistle to the Corinthians*, 608.

30. BDAG, s.v. "συνείδησις." See Thiselton, *First Epistle to the Corinthians*, 640–44. See Witherington, *Conflict and Community*, 199. This also anticipates the later discussion regarding συνείδησις (*syneidēsis*) in 1 Cor 10:28–29.

31. The exception is in 1 Cor 11:30.

Moreover, the Weak have Christ on their side to such an extent that any sin against them is akin to sinning against Christ (8:12).

This is not, therefore, a mere caution to the Knowledgeable to refrain from behavior which may trouble the (misguided) moral faculty of the fragile. Rather, Paul here "springs a rhetorical trap on his audience"[32]—the Weak have been correct to avoid temple dining the whole time. Ciampa and Rosner explain why:

> The problem is not with the food per se, nor merely with the conscience of "weaker brothers," but with any association with idolatry . . . and the risk of leading others, by example, into idolatry . . . The "knowledgeable" Corinthians do not realize that they are in danger of leading other believers to commit subjective idolatry and that they themselves are in danger of committing objective idolatry despite their touted knowledge of monotheism.[33]

By *subjective*, Ciampa and Rosner mean a conscious participation in an idolatrous activity, and by *objective*, they mean someone who participates in an idolatrous activity but without identifying it as such.[34] Such a conceptual framework explains Paul's opposition to the Knowledgeable, whose idolatry is objective, and his concern for the so-called Weak, who may be tempted to return in a consciously subjective sense to their pagan pasts.

Paul's protest against objective idolatry finds completion in 1 Cor 10:1–22 where aspects of the ontological debate in 1 Cor 8:4 feature again (10:20).[35] This time, however, Paul does not appeal to a consequentialist ethic but rather refutes it through a competing claim that involvement in such meals is a participation at the table of demons (10:20–21). While the traditional interpretation argues

32. Perkins, *First Corinthians*, 116.

33. Ciampa and Rosner, *First Letter to the Corinthians*, 369. See Nash, *1 Corinthians*, 238; Bender, *1 Corinthians*, §8.

34. Ciampa and Rosner, *First Letter to the Corinthians*, 369.

35. Contra Dickson, *Mission-Commitment*, 237–47. John Fotopoulos analyzes the literary correspondence between 1 Cor 8 and 10 in the following terms: (1) 1 Cor 8:1–3 and 8:10–9:27; (2) 8:4–7 and 10:14–22; (3) 8:8a and 10:1–13; (4) 8:8b–9 and 10:23—11:1. See Fotopoulos, "Arguments Concerning Food," 619.

that this scenario is distinct from that of dining in an idol's temple (8:4–13), there are no internal literary reasons for thinking so. Yes, Paul does, in 1 Cor 9, undertake an excursus on his apostolic example, but this is in keeping with the theme of relinquishing one's "right" for the salvific well-being of others. There are no literary markers that indicate that Paul then shifts to a different sacred context when he recommences his discussion regarding idolatry from 1 Cor 10:1. It is only from 1 Cor 10:23 that we detect a change of pace and explicit references to scenarios that are distinct from food which is consumed within the sacred precinct of a temple.

If this interpretation is correct, the question of rhetoric remains: Why is Paul uncompromising in his prohibition of idol-food in 1 Cor 10:14–22, whereas in 1 Cor 8 he merely appeals to an accommodation ethic? Richard Hays answers:

> The two arguments are complementary rather than antithetical. Both lead to the same conclusion: Do not go to the temple feasts. By beginning with the argument for building up the community in love, Paul seizes the occasion to teach gnōsis-boasters a lesson they sorely need to learn.[36]

This lesson of love is not simply taught by appealing to consequences for the Weak but is conveyed through Paul's ontological "sparring" with the Corinthians' slogans. Paul, in 1 Cor 8:6, incorporates a Christological confession into the Shema, calling to mind the associated double love command (Deut 6:4–5; Lev 19:18; see Mark 12:29–31). Such love forms the basis of true knowledge (1 Cor 8:3), providing the ontological framework for the type of love that will not only serve the salvific welfare of others but will survive the eschaton (13:13).[37] In other words, Paul's monotheistic vision cultivates in his readers a love for God which seeks the building up of others (8:1) while also anticipating the rejection of idolatry (10:14).

36. Hays, *First Corinthians*, 170–71.

37. Wright, *Climax of the Covenant*, 127.

In summary, the salvific peril that Paul warns against in both 1 Cor 8 and 10 is multifaceted. Those with "knowledge," despite their views to the contrary, are participating in real idolatrous activities associated with pagan temples. Others are now reconsidering their previous dissociation from such temple contexts because of the self-proclaimed "freedom" of the Knowledgeable. That they are in two minds over this matter draws the unjust label of being "weak." So, Paul rebukes the Knowledgeable and defends the reluctance of the Weak. He will later overturn the ill-conceived ontological maxims of the Knowledgeable by declaring that temple dining is participation with demons! In the meantime, however, Paul refrains from such prohibition so that he can first emphasize an ethic of love that seeks the salvific welfare of others.[38] While the initial context is necessarily within the church, this accommodation ethic will be widened in 1 Cor 9 as Paul outlines his own missional ethos. He draws from the motif of *right* (*exousia*, 9:4–6, 12, 18) to provide an alternative vision of becoming a servant of all—even the Weak—so that he might save some (9:22). This Pauline accommodation ethic echoes and extends that which was previously laid down and anticipates a wider missional expression which the Corinthians are to imitate (10:23—11:1).

PAUL'S SALVIFIC COMMITMENT IN 1 COR 9

While the methodology of this study has prioritized an investigation from below which focuses on the missional expectations that Paul places upon the believing community, in 1 Cor 9 he connects his own apostolic mission with this ecclesial ethic of accommodation. Whereas the Knowledgeable make full use of their perceived right (*exousia*, 8:9), Paul employs this same term to offer an alternative vision: "That in preaching the gospel I may offer it free of charge, and so not make full use of my rights [*exousia*] as a preacher of the gospel" (1 Cor 9:18; see 9:4–6, 12). Whereas the Knowledgeable are ruining the Weak (8:11, 13), Paul casts a competing

---

38. Even where this summary is disputed and the traditional view preferred, the overall point of intra-ecclesial salvific intentionality stands.

salvific strategy of becoming weak, in order to win them (9:22). This observation reinforces a critical aspect of this study—that salvific intentionality is directed towards the nurture of insiders as well as towards the conversion of outsiders.[39] Johannes Nissen makes the point that "Paul never thinks of conversion as an end in itself. Each individual has to be continually 're-won' for Christ."[40] This language of rights and weakness indicates the literary interdependence between chapters 8 and 9 and points to the way in which Paul offers his own apostleship as an example for the intraecclesial posture which he has outlined in 1 Cor 8.

Paul's summary of his whole apostolic missionary career in 1 Cor 9:19–23 is widely acknowledged (along with 10:31—11:1) as pivotal to scholarly assessments of Pauline missiology.[41] O'Brien provides a succinct summary in terms of (1) Paul's status as free in Christ; (2) his goal of salvation expressed through the synonymous verbs κερδαίνω (*kerdainō*, "to gain") and σῴζω (*sōzō*, "to save") (9:19–22); (3) the wide range of contexts in which he was socially flexible; and (4) his overall stance of servanthood: "Paul makes himself a slave."[42] Such servanthood is in contradiction to the Corinthians' ethos of freedom (10:23; 6:12). Dustin Ellington highlights the importance of Paul's use of the first person throughout this apostolic summary (9:19–23) and the way in which the language of participation (συγκοινωνός, *synkoinōnos*, 9:23) immediately follows: It is as Paul himself wins people that he "thereby

39. This was also the contention of Bowers, "Church and Mission in Paul," 105. See Barram, *Mission and Moral Reflection*, 14–30. For an argument that it is unlikely that Paul refers here to weak Christians, see Witherington, *Conflict and Community*, 213.

40. Nissen, *New Testament and Mission*, 110. However, Chambers overstates the case in his argument that Paul is "primarily addressing . . . concerns internal to the Corinthian Christian community, not matters pertaining to his (or his converts') relationship to non-Christians." See Chambers, "Paul, His Converts," 139–40.

41. Barram, "Pauline Mission as Salvific Intentionality," 235. See O'Brien, *Consumed by Passion*, 92–107; Nissen, *New Testament and Mission*, 107.

42. O'Brien, *Consumed by Passion*, 99; see 92–107.

participates in the gospel's power and becomes its partner."[43] This salvific intentionality is repeated in the concluding summary in 1 Cor 10:33—11:1 where Paul's example is presented as an ideal to be imitated. In both cases, the identities of ethnic groups in addition to the "church of God"—Jews ('Ιουδαῖοι, *Ioudaioi*) and Greeks ("Ελληνες, *Hellēnes*) (9:20–21; 10:32)—widen the scope of mission consciousness to include the entire world. This raises the prospect that the example of Paul's own accommodation ethic is intended to widen the previous intra-ecclesial concerns in 1 Cor 8, inviting the Corinthians to encompass a salvific concern for outsiders that is parallel to Paul's participation and partnership in the gospel's power.[44] This possibility will be explored in the following section where sourcing meat from the market and social engagement with a pagan host is outlined, after which an analysis will follow of the imitation pattern of Christ–Paul–Corinthians.

SALVIFIC OPPORTUNITIES TOWARDS OUTSIDERS IN 1 COR 10:23–30

While some commentators consider 1 Cor 10:23 as commencing the summary of the entire literary unit to this point (from 8:1),[45] this fails to recognize the introduction of two new scenarios: the market (μάκελλον, *makellon*, 10:25–26) and being the guest of an unbeliever (ἄπιστος, *apistos*, 10:27–28). Knowing that such scenarios were so vital to the economic and social welfare of his readers, it is unsurprising that Paul should address them in view of his previous prohibition of idolatry. The twice-quoted Corinthian

43. Ellington, "Imitating Paul's Relationship," 309.

44. Brian Rosner argues that Paul's expectation that the Corinthians materially support Paul's (and others') traveling ministry is evident from 1 Cor 9:3–14 and 16:6, 10–11 (see 1 Thess 2:1–9), on which see Rosner, "Missionary Character of 1 Corinthians," 185. This is further evidence that Paul assumed a worldwide reference for the Corinthians' salvific concerns, at least as it was to be expressed through supporting Paul and others.

45. Dickson, *Mission-Commitment*, 240–41; Collins, *First Corinthians*, 383. Others see it as a transition to introduce a recapitulation section that then deals with certain objections he anticipated, on which see Nash, *1 Corinthians*, 301.

slogan "I have the right to do anything" (10:23) and subsequent rebuttals (ἀλλά, *alla*, "but") echo those previously offered (6:12; 8:1) and pave the way for the restatement of Paul's ethic, grounded in love and ordered for the salvific good of the other: "No one should seek their own good, but the good of others" (10:24; see 5:5; 8:1, 9, 13; 9:19–23; 12:7; 14:3). While in 1 Cor 8 this good was articulated as an intra-ecclesial accommodation ethic, Paul's expression of his own apostolic practice now extends this accommodation ethic to encompass all: "I have become all things to all people so that by all possible means I might save some" (9:22). In the summary proper (10:33—11:1) Paul will frame the scope of this goal as an example for the Corinthians to imitate. This makes it likely that the imperative to "seek the . . . good of others" (1 Cor 10:24), which introduces the market and guest scenarios, is informed not simply by the intra-ecclesial ethic of 1 Cor 8 but also by the extended scope of Paul's intentions expressed in 1 Cor 9. In other words, by introducing the two scenarios in terms of "seek the . . . good of others," Paul is referencing his own example and thus extending the accommodation ethic of 1 Cor 8 to encompass outsiders.

The first scenario is that of sourcing food, likely meat, from the market (10:25). The issue here is not that of sacred space but of sacred origin. With cultic meat entering the general marketplace, it may have been difficult for the shopper to distinguish between it and non-sacred food.[46] Or, it could be that Paul is envisioning the consumption of food provided secondhand by another (as in the subsequent scenario) who has purchased it from the market. Whatever the exact circumstances, David Garland states it playfully: "Christ has not called them to be meat inspectors."[47] The freedom to eat everything sold at the market, without any investigation as to its sacred origin, is reinforced by the participial phrase μηδὲν ἀνακρίνοντες διὰ τὴν συνείδησιν (*mēden anakrinontes dia tēn syneidēsin*), "without asking about it because of your self-awareness" (10:25).[48] While some suggest that this is Paul's invitation

46. Smith, *From Symposium to Eucharist*, 84.

47. Garland, *1 Corinthians*, 490.

48. This translation relies upon Thiselton, *First Epistle to the Corinthians*,

to the Weak to be less scrupulous about idol meat, this is unlikely since it is the slogan of the Knowledgeable that introduces this section (10:23). More likely, Paul is laying down some practical principles of social engagement in view of the vigor with which he has prohibited food associated with idolatry up to this point (8:12; 10:21). This reinforces the view that the reference here to συνείδησις (*syneidēsis*) pertains to consciousness or self-awareness regarding this information.[49] Indeed, the consciousness in view, while referencing the Christian eater in the first instance, antici-pates the scenario to come in which it is the consciousness of the other that is at stake (10:28–29). In this first scenario, however, Paul is adopting a generous integrationist principle: that food from the market can be consumed without inquiry as to its sacred origin because it falls within the sacred space of the Lord.

The quotation from Ps 24:1, "The earth is the Lord's, and ev-erything in it" (1 Cor 10:26), introduces a more ultimate sacred space which trumps the so-called sacred origin of food from the markets and households of Corinth. Psalm 24 describes Yahweh's temple as a symbol of divine sovereignty and that which indicates that all of creation belongs to the Lord. Here Paul's reasoning reso-nates with the divine declaration that all food is considered clean (Acts 10:9–16; Mark 7:18–19) and provides a theological basis for what the Knowledgeable have previously claimed regarding the in-significance of food (1 Cor 8:8). The resisting tendencies required in sacred precincts are replaced with the integrating tendencies of sharing in the common marketplace in Corinth (10:25) and as the guest of a pagan host (10:27). This freedom, however, can be inter-rupted by the consciousness of another, whose salvific welfare the Corinthians are to seek. Such a possibility is introduced in the next scenario where an interjector alerts the Christian guest that their food has idolatrous association.

There is no internal evidence that the unbeliever's invita-tion in 1 Cor 10:27 involves the Christian attending an idolatrous

---

784–85.

49. BDAG, s.v. "συνείδησις." See Witherington, *Conflict and Community*, 199.

sacred space.[50] The presence of idol-food (10:28) makes it certain that the identity of the unbelieving (*apistos*, 10:27) host is a pagan outsider—those with whom Paul expected the believing community to maintain social contact (5:9–13; 7:12–16; see 10:20–25). Paul outlines a scenario in which an interjector declares the idolatrous association of the food. It is generally agreed that the use of the non-polemical term for idol-food (ἱερόθυτόν, *hierothyton*, 10:28) indicates that it is a pagan who has alerted the Christian to this reality.[51] Perhaps it was a customary part of the meal experience in which a deity was invoked. Or it was the host himself or a fellow guest who had sympathy towards the Christian's religious affiliation. During a banquet various dishes were provided,[52] only some of which may have had a sacred association, providing the Christian with a means of temporarily opting out without causing unnecessary offence to the host.[53] The reason for not partaking of such food is not for the sake of the informant, as if to imply that it will subjectively trouble them, but *because* of (διά, *dia* with the accusative) him or her. What is ambiguous, though, is whether it is the consciousness (συνείδησις, *syneidēsis*) of this informant that is then mentioned or if there is another person who is also in view:

> v. 28b: μὴ ἐσθίετε δι' ἐκεῖνον τὸν μηνύσαντα καὶ τὴν συνείδησιν·
>
> *mē esthiete di' ekeinon ton mēnysanta kai tēn syneidēsin;*

50. Contra Dickson, *Mission-Commitment*, 243. Indeed, Paul has commenced this literary subunit not in the temple but in the marketplace. In a city the size of Corinth such markets would have existed in various places around the city, on which see Winter, *After Paul Left Corinth*, 302.

51. Dickson, *Mission-Commitment*, 244. Witherington, *Conflict and Community*, 227; Fee, *First Epistle to the Corinthians*, 482–83; Nash, *1 Corinthians*, 304. Chambers' insistence that the informant could be a weak Christian using the gentile term out of social appropriateness is possible but speculative. See Chambers, "Paul, His Converts," 156, 169.

52. Sallares, "Meals," 916.

53. Ciampa and Rosner, *First Letter to the Corinthians*, 492. For a treatment of idol-food in social meals at private homes see Cheung, *Idol Food in Corinth*, 33–34. See Witherington, *Conflict and Community*, 191–95.

v. 29a: συνείδησιν δὲ λέγω οὐχὶ τὴν ἑαυτοῦ ἀλλὰ τὴν τοῦ ἑτέρου.

syneidēsin de legō ouchi tēn heautou alla tēn tou heterou.

Dickson argues that ἑαυτοῦ (*heautou*) in 1 Cor 10:29a ought to be read as a third-person singular possessive pronoun whose antecedent is the informant: "The consciousness, I say, not of the one who informed you, but of the other."[54] While this is grammatically possible, it is just as likely that καί (*kai*) in 1 Cor 10:28b does not identify a separate entity but functions in an ascensive or explanatory sense: "Do not eat on account of the informant, namely [their] consciousness."[55] The following clause (10:29a) therefore confirms Paul's intent that the informant is the catalyst for abstaining from eating: "not your consciousness, I say, but that of the informant."[56] Again, the meaning of συνείδησις (*syneidēsis*) is not an internal moral conflict (after all, why would a pagan be conflicted in such circumstances?) but an awareness or consciousness of what is at stake. Paul's objection in such a scenario is consistent with what Jewish halakah regulations of the time specified: "Eating what a pagan appears to consider an offering to his deity signifies cooperation in idolatry."[57]

54. Thus, Dickson posits that the other (ἑαυτοῦ) "casts us back to the situation of 8:10ff. in which a weak believer . . . observes the 'knowledgeable' one eating in a sacred precinct . . . Here, as there, it is the συνείδησιν (8:10b/10:29a) of the 'other,' weak as it is through lack of knowledge, that leads to dangerous consequences and provides the reason for refraining from eating." See Dickson, *Mission-Commitment*, 246. As has been argued, against such a reading is that 1 Cor 10:23–30 is not a summary of the preceding section, nor is it a sacred temple setting, and there are no explicit literary links with the Knowledgeable (nor the Strong) and the Weak in this latter section.

55. My translation. This reading then understands 1 Cor 10:29b–30 as a parenthetical clause, which functions as a diatribe that reinforces that it is the other person's consciousness which defines the issue, not Paul's own. In other words, he can freely partake of idol-food if the origin of it is not pointed out as is the case in 1 Cor 10:25–26.

56. My translation.

57. Tomson, *Paul and the Jewish Law*, 216–19.

That Paul specifies the awareness of the informant as the critical feature of this scenario is simply to emphasize that the catalyst should not be the believer's inquiry but an explicit declaration of idolatrous intent that requires the believer to refrain from any such involvement. To continue with this part of the meal would be a participation in forbidden idolatry, which would, according to Garland, "compromise their confession of the one true God with a tacit recognition of the sanctity of pagan gods."[58] Equally, and emphatically in the text, the awareness of the interjector is also important but obviously for different reasons. Dickson explains that the Christian is to act in the salvific interests of the "aware" pagan:

> Participation by a Christian in a meal explicitly devoted (by public announcement) to a Greek deity presents a potential, albeit implicit, affirmation of the non-Christian's idolatrous beliefs. Such an affirmation lays an obstacle ($\dot{\alpha}\pi\rho\acute{o}\sigma\kappa\sigma\tau\sigma\varsigma$ in v. 32) in the pagan's path to 'true piety.' Whatever the social consequences of declining to partake of such a meal, the critique of paganism implied in this course of action contains significant mission possibilities, providing an opportunity for the apologetic slogans of the Corinthian church—"no idol in the world really exists" (8:4b); " there is no God but one" (8:4c) . . . to be publicly embodied, and perhaps even aired, in a pagan setting. Such an affirmation will, in the view of Paul, glorify God (10:31) and work for the benefit of others that they may be saved (10:33).[59]

That Paul considers it important to address this household dining scenario is once again indicative of the importance of social meals in Greco-Roman society.[60] The nature of reciprocity may have also opened opportunities for believers to successfully

---

58. Garland, *1 Corinthians*, 497. See Witherington, *Conflict and Community*, 227–28.

59. Dickson, *Mission-Commitment*, 245.

60. Gooch sets out three aspects: "food as a marker of social distinction, meals as social requirements and shared meals as expressions of friendships." See Gooch, *Dangerous Food*, 38.

invite their pagan neighbors to Christian gatherings[61]—such a scenario will be explored in the following chapter. Although it is common to emphasize Roman hostility to the early Christian movement, there is little evidence of such conflict in 1 Corinthians itself. Indeed, many of Paul's efforts consist in nurturing a sense of group boundaries that balance an integrating affinity with resistance tendencies.[62] Thus, it is entirely possible, given the internal indicators of social ease between group identities, that religious conversations may have occurred at such meals, either when the Christian was a guest or if a reciprocal invitation was extended with the believer as the host.

This social reality challenges a particular methodological approach to the apparent absence of ecclesial mission first raised in the introductory chapter. There has, in my view, been a category error when missiology has been narrowly categorized into active (e.g., verbal proclamation) or passive (e.g., godly living) expressions of mission-commitment.[63] Such distinctions do not adequately account for the social realities of the ancient world in which the ethical distinctives of early Christianity would have necessarily invited and required verbal explanations. Indeed, Greco-Roman dining culture included table talk where religious topics, along with political and philosophical discussion, were standard components of the symposium.[64] The ethical and verbal missionary possibilities of any such dining scenario is given more explicit endorsement in the climactic unit which features next.

SALVIFIC IMITATION IN 1 COR 10:31—11:1

The inferential οὖν (*oun*, "therefore") commences the climactic summary of the entire literary unit beginning at 1 Cor 8:1, drawing an explicit connection between an intra-ecclesial accommodation

61. Dickson, *Mission-Commitment*, 261.

62. Tucker, "Role of Civic Identity," 73–75.

63. Bowers, "Church and Mission in Paul," 89–111.

64. Witherington, *Community and Conflict*, 193; see Gooch, *Dangerous Food*, 27–38.

ethic, Paul's apostleship, and the wider missional consciousness expected of the believing community. The exhortation to eat and drink for God's glory (1 Cor 10:31) stands in contrast to the pagan idolatrous worship addressed in 1 Cor 8 and 10, so much of which was associated with dining experiences. The verbal cognate of δόξα (*doxa*, "glory") previously occurred in 1 Cor 6:19–20 in close association with temple imagery. The Corinthian assembly constitutes an alternative sacred space to the temples in Corinth—it is "the temple of God in which the Spirit of God dwells."[65] Indeed, Ps 24, the first verse of which is quoted in 1 Cor 10:26, is a temple Psalm in which the king of glory (δόξα, *doxa*, LXX Ps 23:7–10) is recognized as the one who inhabits his temple and lays claim to the possession of the entire world. No longer, for Paul, does God dwell in Zion but among his people, even the Corinthians (1 Cor 3:16–17), who serve, in part, as the fulfillment of a prophetic tradition that anticipates the temple as the means of the eschatological inclusion of the gentiles (1 Cor 1:2; see Mal 1:11; Hag 2:7).[66] Thus, the Corinthians are themselves the result of the missiological purpose of the temple, and as members of this new temple they are to take up the priestly vocation of Israel to promote God's reputation among the nations (Exod 19:3–6).[67] Brian Rosner points out the significance of Isa 66:18–24 on Paul's missiological reflections:

> There is both an "outward" and "inward" dynamic to God's glorification: God's glory will be declared to the nations by missionaries (v. 19), and the nations will come and glorify God in temple worship (vv. 18, 23). The eschatological remnant will act as priests in God's temple in Jerusalem (v. 20), bringing those scattered among the nations as an offering to the Lord.[68]

---

65. Suh, *Power and Peril*, §2.7. Kar Yong Lim rightly recognizes that the temple metaphor extends, at least in the mind of Paul's readers, to the reality of the temples in Corinth. However, he under-appreciates the eschatological and missiological implications of the Old Testament temple imagery for Paul himself. See Lim, *Metaphors and Social Identity*, §5.

66. Ciampa and Rosner, *First Letter to the Corinthians*, 57–58.

67. Beale, *Temple and the Church's Mission*, 400.

68. Rosner, "Glory of God," 160–61.

It is for this reason that Paul has closely identified the Corinthian community with that of Israel (1 Cor 10:1–13), exhorting them to faithful worship (10:14–22) and outlining two scenarios (the meat market, 10:25; and being a guest of a pagan host, 10:27) which bear upon the reputation of the Lord.

That glorifying God is closely connected with salvific concerns for others is demonstrated in what immediately follows. Two imperatival clauses "sandwich" Paul's apostolic example of seeking the salvific welfare of all (10:33):

> 10:32   Do not cause anyone to stumble, whether Jews, Greeks or the church of God.
>
> 11:1   Follow my example, as I follow the example of Christ.

Fee points out that ἀπρόσκοπος (*aproskopos*, "not stumble," 10:32) is the negative form of the noun πρόσκομμα (*proskomma*, "stumble") which Paul previously used in 1 Cor 8:9 to reference behavior that imperiled the salvation of one's fellow believer (see 8:11–13).[69] Now, however, avoidance of such negative possibilities is not just an intra-ecclesial matter but "casts the net as widely as possible"[70] by encompassing a concern for the Jews and Greeks in addition to the church of God (10:32).[71] Such differentiation constitutes what Denise Buell calls *ethnic reasoning*:

> Early Christians used ethnic reasoning to legitimize various forms of Christianness as the universal, most authentic manifestation of humanity, and it offered Christians both a way to define themselves relative to "outsiders" and to compete with other "insiders" to assert the superiority of their varying visions of Christianness.[72]

This explicit identification of ethnic group identities "outside" the church, towards whom the Corinthians have a salvific responsibility, is then connected (καθώς, *kathōs*, "just as") to Paul's own

69. Fee, *First Epistle to the Corinthians*, 488n63.

70. Ciampa and Rosner, *First Letter to the Corinthians*, 496.

71. Contra Chambers, "Paul, His Converts," 143.

72. Buell, *Why This New Race*, 2.

example (10:33). This pithy summary draws from 1 Cor 9:19–23 where already the Jews (9:20) and the gentiles (9:21) have been identified as the object of his apostolic commission. Whereas in 9:22 the rhetoric of salvific intentionality is described from Paul's own first-person perspective, the summary in 10:33 describes only the intention of pleasing and profiting in such terms, before switching to the divine passive rendering of salvific outcomes: "so that they may be saved" (ἵνα σωθῶσιν, *hina sōthōsin*). This does not in any way lessen expectations of salvific intentionality but can be understood as a reflection of Paul's desire to incorporate into this summary what he had previously framed in terms of his partnership in the gospel, that is, the action of God through Paul and now, by extension, through his readers (9:23).[73]

The second part of the imperatival "sandwich" (11:1) is, in Hays's view, the "climax" of the literary unit.[74] In what way does Paul expect his readers to imitate him? Chambers is content to narrow Paul's salvific aims in 1 Cor 10:33 to "a desire that all of his converts should continue in the salvation they had already received."[75] Bowers attaches the pattern of imitation not so much to the scope of Paul's mission but to a form that is to be replicated within the community of faith:

> The primary line of action Paul is urging in the text concerns not an evangelistic outreach to unbelievers but a voluntary self-renunciation within the life of the community . . . what is involved here is not an incentive to active witness, to an evangelistic campaign, but an incentive so to shape one's conduct that it does not prove a hindrance to the attraction of unbelievers.[76]

Most scholars, however, acknowledge that imitation here refers to both behavior and intentionality and encompasses not simply "the church of God" but those two ethnic identities, distinct

---

73. Schütz, *Paul and the Anatomy of Apostolic Authority*, 230.

74. Hays, *First Corinthians*, 179.

75. Chambers, "Paul, His Converts," 144.

76. Bowers, "Church and Mission in Paul," 94.

from it, which together refer to the entire world.[77] The Corinthians are called to imitate both the form and scope of Paul's missionary concerns. This is not to suggest that Paul intended his converts to engage in the same missionary initiatives as himself—clearly Paul recognized differentiation in roles, commissioning, and gifts. Yet there is a pattern of salvific intention that believers are to imitate, and it reaches back through Paul to Christ himself. Dickson entertains the possibility that Paul's summary, which commences with eating and drinking (10:31), may allude to Jesus' own missional habit of eating and drinking with sinners (Luke 7:34).[78] Bailey identifies the same form of words in Luke 10:8 where the Seventy are sent out.[79] While such are possibilities, Barram points out that it is "Christ" language that is invoked:

> [Paul] does not refer to Jesus of Nazareth, as if he were appealing primarily to the Messiah's terrestrial behavior as an example. Paul is concerned primarily here with "the Christ," the one whom the apostle regularly characterizes in soteriological terms. "Christ," according to Paul, consistently acted "for us" . . . Christ demonstrated unrelenting commitment to the criterion of salvation with regard to behavior . . . . The apostle imitates Christ. If the Corinthian Christians imitate him, their behavior will be based on the appropriate criterion: the salvation of others.[80]

Thus, in Paul's climactic imitation appeal, the readers are reminded of the cosmic scope of the Christ's impact upon both Jew and Greek of this age (1:17–25), the way in which this shaped

---

77. Ellington, "Imitating Paul's Relationship," 313; Barram, *Mission and Moral Reflection*, 70–71; O'Brien, *Consumed by Passion*, 97–99; Dickson, *Mission-Commitment*, 253.

78. Dickson, *Mission-Commitment*, 254.

79. Bailey, *Paul through Mediterranean Eyes*, 292. For a suggestion that Isaiah's suffering servant is alluded to, see Ciampa and Rosner, *First Letter to the Corinthians*, 498.

80. Barram, *Mission and Moral Reflection*, 75–76.

Paul's apostolic self-understanding, and thus their own horizontal participation in the salvific activity of their God and Christ.[81]

CONCLUSION

The form and scope of salvific intentionality are inseparable. It finds its genesis in the mission of the eschatological Christ whose death for our sins (1 Cor 15:3) and resurrection as the last Adam (15:45) recasts theological identity and invites both Jew and Greek to be incorporated into the church of God. Thus, the mission of the believing community cannot be limited to those of insider-identity only. The mission of Christ has incorporated the Corinthians, although they were once outsiders! As those now included in this insider temple identity, the believing community itself is the means through which more Jews and Greeks will be saved.

It is important, however, to draw a distinction between the common mission in which Christ, Paul, and the Corinthians share and the particular expression that each party will undertake. Such expressions evident in 1 Cor 8:1—11:1 include an intra-ecclesial accommodation ethic intended to build up fellow believers and prevent their salvific ruin. Moreover, Paul highlights his own application of this accommodation ethic as he seeks the salvation of all—both Jew and gentile (1 Cor 9:19–23). This expanded scope of salvific intentionality then frames two scenarios in which the Corinthians' social integration, whether at the market or as guests in pagan households, is to be "harnessed for missionary effect" (10:23–30).[82]

In the introductory chapter, brief reference was made to passive and active categories for describing ecclesial mission-commitment. The scenarios discussed in this chapter demonstrate the limitations of such language that typically construe verbal proclamation as an active expression of mission and other forms

81. Consider also, so far in the letter, these Christological effects: 1 Cor 1:13, 17; 5:7; 6:20; 8:11. Also consider how this Christ language anticipates further references: 1 Cor 11:17–26; 15:3–6.

82. Dickson, *Mission-Commitment*, 259.

such as godly living as passive. Indeed, the verbal interjection at the home of the pagan in 1 Cor 10:28 presupposes, and invites, verbal responses of a socioreligious nature—the Greco-Roman dining culture expected as much. This threshold of evidence is like that found in 1 Cor 7:12–16 where believers in a mixed marriage are expected to negotiate (presumably with their words) their living arrangements with their spouse, in view of their newfound religious commitment. In other words, when approached from below, in terms of the missional expectations that Paul places upon his readers, it becomes evident that verbal explanations of their Christian faith commitment necessarily go hand in hand with their resisting behaviors regarding idolatry. Indeed, in the next chapter, the nature of the Corinthians' speech features as the determining factor for an outsider's rejection or acceptance of the claims of Christianity.

4

Salvific Intentionality in the Gathering

1 Cor 14:20–25

MANY FEATURES OF THE discussion so far come together in this forthcoming analysis of 1 Cor 14:20–25. Although the actual verb σῴζω (*sōzō*, "to save") is absent, Paul uses salvific imagery to emphasize the effect of certain speech-modes upon those at a Corinthian gathering, including unbelievers who may be present. From 1 Cor 14:1 Paul develops a contrast between γλῶσσαι (*glōssai*, hereafter "tongues") and προφητεία (*prophēteia*, hereafter "prophecy") summarized in 14:22 as two principles related to their gatherings, and I paraphrase:[1]

Tongues are the speech-mode of *faithless* Israel/Corinth.

Prophecy is the speech-mode of *faithful* Israel/Corinth.

Paul then reinforces these principles by appealing to a scenario in which outsiders may come into the gathering. Whereas tongues have an alienating effect upon them, prophecy results in what

1. The credibility of this paraphrase will be part of the developing argument of this chapter.

Dickson calls an "idealized portrait of conversion":[2] "So they will fall down and worship God, exclaiming, 'God is really among you!'" (14:25).

Curiously, two types of outsiders are specified in 1 Cor 14:23–25: ἰδιῶται (*idiōtai*) and ἄπιστοι (*apistoi*). While the latter describe unbelievers, the former are more ambiguous, appearing in the prior section as those unable to understand tongues (14:16). Although ἰδιώτης (*idiōtēs*) refers to an "amateur" or one who is "unskilled," in this context it identifies "one not knowledgeable about a particular group's experience"—an inside outsider of sorts, at least from the perspective of some within the community.[3] Hence Thiselton suggests the term *ungifted*, at least as far as the "spiritual" ones in Corinth regard those without tongues.[4]

That the Corinthian church includes various such groups has been an important observation throughout this study. Once again, in the words of Lang, the premise of Paul's letter was, at least in part, "to distinguish between types of insiders" and to respond in a suitable way to the untidy social circumstances of the church.[5] Part of Paul's response is to develop and cultivate his readers' salvific consciousness that they might build up their fellow believers and seek the salvation of the outsider. A complementary aspect of this study has been to notice evidence of integrating social tendencies between the believing community and its wider connections within Corinth. Not only did Paul expect such association, but previous chapters have analyzed texts which assume the relative normality of mixed marriage and the complex socioreligious context of idol-food. In both cases, unbelieving outsiders maintain significant and ongoing contact with insiders. This insider-outsider association may explain why Paul, in 1 Cor 14:23–25, continues his emphasis

---

2. Dickson, *Mission-Commitment*, 300.

3. BDAG, s.v. "ἰδιώτης."

4. Thiselton, *First Epistle to the Corinthians*, 1115. Regarding tongues functioning as a status indicator of those who considered themselves spiritually superior, see Thiselton, *First Epistle to the Corinthians*, 1074–77.

5. Lang, "Trouble with Insiders," 981–82.

on salvific intentionality even in the context of Christian gatherings which occur in the domestic spaces of believers.

This untidy social profile of the Corinthians is an important consideration in resolving a long-standing conundrum in this text. Having asserted that "tongues, then, are a sign, not for believers but for unbelievers" and that "prophecy . . . is not for unbelievers but for believers" (14:22), Paul subsequently, and apparently, demonstrates just the opposite (14:23–25). I say *apparently* because the so-called contradiction is resolved, in my view, when the sociotheological identities of the various groups are clarified. The argument anticipated in the earlier paraphrase of 1 Cor 14:22 is that Paul assumes a distinction within the people of God—insiders may be categorized in terms of *faithless* and *faithful*. This, as far as I am aware, is a unique explanation of 1 Cor 14:22.

Interpreted along the lines I outline below, 1 Cor 14:20–25 demonstrates the comprehensive way in which Paul commends and nurtures the salvific intentions of his converts in their relationships within their community and towards outsiders. This chapter will proceed with an analysis of the structure and meaning of Paul's argument with reference to the wider literary unit commencing from 1 Cor 14:1. These findings will then inform an analysis of the socioreligious nature of Corinthian gatherings and the potential relationship between prophecy and any outsider groups present. In outlining such salvific outcomes, Paul brings the important theme of Isaiah's temple to its fulfillment, showing that such prophecy, in the Corinthian gatherings, is indicative of the restoration of Israel.

PAUL'S ARGUMENT IN 1 COR 14:20–25

Despite the lack of scholarly consensus on almost every point in these five verses, I contend that close attention to the following critical questions will reveal Paul's coherent argument: (1) the significance of Isa 28:11–12 in its initial context and then in Paul's argument; (2) the meaning of σημεῖον (*sēmeion*, "sign"); (3) the sociotheological identity of the various "groups" within the pericope; and (4) how specific points correspond with Paul's wider tongues/prophecy discourse (14:1–40). I propose that 1 Cor 14:22 is the concluding principle that Paul's unfolding argument (from 14:1) has been moving towards. The subsequent scenario where outsiders enter the assembly is not the climax of Paul's argument but rather the "icing on the cake"—the reinforcing proof of Paul's prior conclusion. The internal logic of Paul's argument may be outlined as follows:

Appeal (v. 20):	Be mature.
Premise (v. 21):	Despite Assyrian tongues, Israel remained faithless (Isa 28:11–12).
Conclusion A (v. 22a):	Tongues are a sign of unbelieving Israel/Corinth.
Conclusion B (v. 22b):	Prophecy is a sign of believing Israel/Corinth.
Further proof A (v. 23):	The negative salvific effect of Corinthian tongues upon ἰδιῶται ἢ ἄπιστοι (*idiōtai ē apistoi*).
Further proof B (vv. 24–25):	The positive salvific effect of Corinthian prophecy upon τις ἄπιστος ἢ ἰδιώτη (*tis apistos ē idiōtē*).

Appeal (1 Cor 14:20)

> Ἀδελφοί, μὴ παιδία γίνεσθε ταῖς φρεσὶν ἀλλὰ τῇ κακίᾳ νηπιάζετε, ταῖς δὲ φρεσὶν τέλειοι γίνεσθε.
>
> *Adelphoi, mē paidia ginesthe tais phresin alla tē kakia nēpiazete, tais de phresin teleioi ginesthe.*
>
> Brothers, do not be children in your understanding, but in respect to evil be infants, and in your understanding be mature.[6]

The language of brothers signals a subtle development in Paul's argument towards a summarizing statement. Beginning in 1 Cor

6. The translation throughout this section is my own.

14:1, the benefit of prophecy has been contrasted with the short-comings associated with tongues. Prophecy corresponds most directly with an ethic of love (14:1) and serves as an intelligible speech-mode (14:9, 19) directed towards the edification, encouragement, and comfort of others (14:3).[7] Tongues, on the other hand, refer to a mysterious speech-mode (14:2), corresponding to one's own spirit (14:14) that, given their orientation towards God (14:2), provides benefit only to oneself (14:4).[8] Even the logic of Paul's "exception clauses" holds true to this fundamental tongues/prophecy contrast. Yes, tongues *are* valid when translated (14:5, 13, 27, 40), but this very act of translation transforms this mysterious speech-mode into that which can be understood, and thus they become analogous to prophecy. It seems from what Paul writes that he sees no place for tongues in the assembly, at least in so far as the Corinthians are practicing them untranslated.

The child/mature contrast in 1 Cor 14:20 corresponds therefore to the preceding tongues/prophecy rhetoric. The familial language of brothers gives way to a shame/honor comparison—rather than being mature, the Corinthians are behaving as children, a criticism which has previously been leveled at them (3:1; see 13:11). Moreover, this reference to children may well echo the wider context of Isa 28:11–12, which will come into focus in the very next verse.[9] The complaint of the religious leaders of Isaiah's

7. This descriptor of προφητεία (*prophēteia*) is sufficient for this study. For a comprehensive review of the literature and possibilities, see Thiselton, *First Epistle to the Corinthians*, 956–65, 1087–94.

8. This descriptor of γλῶσσαι (*glōssai*) is sufficient for this study. For a comprehensive review of the literature and possibilities, see Thiselton, *First Epistle to the Corinthians*, 970–89, 1098–1100. It is likely that tongues are functioning as a status-indicator over the ἰδιῶται (*idiōtai*), on which see Perkins, *First Corinthians*, 156. It is unclear if Paul is simply critical of the *misuse* of tongues, or whether he completely disapproves of their use in the assembly. As noted, the purpose of translation (1 Cor 14:27–28) is to transform this speech-mode into that which is analogous to prophecy. Whether such translation is even possible is opaque to the modern interpreter—perhaps Paul is conceding that translating a tongue would make the practice acceptable while anticipating that such a possibility is unlikely to take place?

9. Kenneth Bailey suggests that this "prophetic homily has obviously been

day was that his message was too simple—it was for children (Isa 28:9–10):

> Who is it he is trying to teach? To whom is he explaining his message? To children weaned from their milk, to those just taken from the breast? For it is: Do this, do that, a rule for this, a rule for that; a little here, a little there.

Paul draws a comparison between the way those leaders demonstrated their own puerile attitude in taunting the prophet (probably drawing on the use of mimicking sounds used for teaching a child the Hebrew alphabet) and that of the Corinthians' childish resistance to his apostolic words.[10] Barry Webb explains, "The drunken leaders mock the word of God through the prophet as infantile nonsense, childish prattle."[11] Similarly, while the Corinthians were critical of Paul's teaching, it was, in fact, *they* who needed to become more mature. This appeal in 1 Cor 14:20 commences a summary of the preceding section (14:1–19), the focus of which is an intra-ecclesial tongues/prophecy contrast. This summary is best understood as reaching its conclusion in 1 Cor 14:22.

Premise (1 Cor 14:21)

> ἐν τῷ νόμῳ γέγραπται ὅτι ἐν ἑτερογλώσσοις καὶ ἐν χείλεσιν ἑτέρων λαλήσω τῷ λαῷ τούτῳ καὶ οὐδ' οὕτως εἰσακούσονταί μου, λέγει κύριος.

> *en tō nomō gegraptai hoti en heteroglōssois kai en cheilesin heterōn lalēsō tō laō toutō kai oud' houtōs eisakousontai mou, legei kyrios.*

---

on Paul's mind at various times during the composition of 1 Corinthians." See Bailey, *Paul through Mediterranean Eyes*, 400.

10. Ciampa and Rosner, *First Letter to the Corinthians*, 697. See Kistemaker, *Exposition*, 499.

11. Webb, *Message of Isaiah*, 120.

> In the Law it is written: "By foreign languages and the lips of others I will speak to this people, and not even then will they listen to me," says the Lord.

Before arriving at the principles which summarize the whole section (14:22), Paul quotes from the law, a term which, in this case, is generic enough to include prophetic writings. Paul's paraphrase of Isa 28:11–12 is from the center of Isaiah's judgment oracle against Israel and her leadership (Isa 28–29). The divine complaint points out the intoxicated state of Israel's priests and prophets who are muddled in their visions and stumble in their judgments (Isa 28:1, 7). In mocking the prophetic word, they fail to hear and obey the clear voice of the Lord, which contains great wisdom (Isa 28:9–10, 14, 22–29). Thus, Paul's loose quotation of Isa 28:11–12 references this first context of divine judgment through foreign invasion—the Assyrian "prattle" which will accompany the covenant curse of exile (Isa 28:2–3, 22; 29:1–8).[12] Elements of this prophetic tradition are shared with Jeremiah (e.g., Jer 5:13–15) who likely draws, along with Isaiah, from an older Deuteronomic tradition in which judgment is associated with invasion by a nation whose language is not understood (Deut 28:45–50).[13] Alec Motyer explains, "When the simple intelligibility of the word of God is refused, divine judgment falls in the shape of the unintelligible."[14] What is vital to recognize, however, is the purpose of such prophetic warnings within the framework of covenant: "It is response seeking."[15] Isaiah's warning regarding this historic threat of pending Assyrian invasion (foreign tongues) was intended to elicit a believing response from Israel, and yet they would not listen (Isa 28:11–12; 1 Cor 14:21). This failure to listen then and, by implication, now (in Paul's day) is why he quotes from Isaiah—the Corinthians are children mocking his apostolic word just as Israel mocked Isaiah's word.

12. Webb, *Message of Isaiah*, 120.

13. Heil, *Rhetorical Role of Scripture*, 202.

14. Motyer, *Prophecy of Isaiah*, 232.

15. Moberly, *Prophecy and Discernment*, 52.

This analysis draws out a critical but under-recognized observation regarding the descriptors that immediately follow the Isaiah quotation: οἱ πιστεύοντες (*hoi pisteuontes*) and οἱ ἄπιστοι (*hoi apistoi*, 14:22)—they apply in the first instance to *the people of God*. As Paul paraphrases Isaiah, he is applying an intra-ecclesial distinction between believing and unbelieving Israel, the faithful and faithless. This is a well-recognized Old Testament tradition, which seeks to provoke a faithful response from within: "Return, faithless Israel" (Jer 3:12; see 6–22;[16] see Deut 29–30; Isa 29:13; Hos 1; 14:1–3; Rom 9–11). Indeed, Isaiah's opening homily is framed in just this way: "Wash and make yourselves clean. Take your evil deeds out of my sight; stop doing wrong . . . . See how the faithful city has become a prostitute!" (Isa 1:16, 21a). This raises the possibility that, as Isaiah addressed those within the covenant people as faithless, Paul may also have been addressing the Corinthian community in these same terms. Such a reading coheres with Paul's use of the cognate verb ἀπιστέω (*apisteō*) in Rom 3:3 in which Paul refers to some within the Jews, who, despite being entrusted with the words of God, were unfaithful/faithless.[17] Thus, Paul seems to employ the adjectival noun (ἄπιστοι, *apistoi*, "unbelieving" or "faithless," my translation) in 1 Cor 14:22 in a way that is different from 14:23–25 where it assumes a more technical outsider identity marker.[18]

In summary so far, Paul's argument against tongues, at least as the Corinthians are practicing them in the assembly, has been intensifying—they fail to edify in 1 Cor 14:1–6, they alienate in 14:6–12, and in 14:12–19 ten thousand of them are no match for five intelligible alternatives. Paul now borrows from Isaiah's message to faithless Israel to issue an analogous warning to faithless Corinth (14:22)—in both cases it is a covenant distinction within the people of God.

16. ἀφίστημι (*aphistēmi*) in LXX Jer 3:14 refers to faithless Israel. See Heb 3:12 and Luke 8:13.

17. 2 Maccabees 8:13 is another use in extant literature that may indicate such an internal reference.

18. Contra Munoz who, although recognizing that the Isaiah citation lends itself to this insider reference in 1 Cor 14:22, argues that "the original reference to unfaithful Israel drops out." See Munoz, "How Not to Go Out," 109–10.

Conclusion A (1 Cor 14:22a) and B (1 Cor 14:22b)

> (A) ὥστε αἱ γλῶσσαι εἰς σημεῖόν εἰσιν οὐ τοῖς πιστεύουσιν ἀλλὰ τοῖς ἀπίστοις, (B) ἡ δὲ προφητεία οὐ τοῖς ἀπίστοις ἀλλὰ τοῖς πιστεύουσιν.

> (A) *hōste hai glōssai eis sēmeion eisin ou tois pisteuousin alla tois apistois,* (B) *hē de prophēteia ou tois apistois alla tois pisteuousin.*

> (A) Therefore, tongues are a sign, not of the faithful, but of the faithless; (B) prophecy, however, is [a sign] not of the faithless but of the faithful.

After reviewing the literature associated with 1 Cor 14:22, Thiselton writes, "This is acknowledged to be one of the most difficult verses in our epistle."[19] There is no scholarly consensus as to its logical connection with the preceding verse and certainly none in terms of the scenario which follows (14:23–25). The long-standing difficulty lies in the perceived contradiction between what Paul states in 1 Cor 14:22 and the reactions attributed to the outsiders in 14:23–25. While my argument has anticipated this apparent contradiction by translating 14:22 in terms of the covenant categories of faithful and faithless Israel/Corinth, the following represents an attempt to review the scholarly discussion and outline the critical concerns.

B. C. Johanson outlines what is at stake when he proposes that 1 Cor 14:22 is a rhetorical question from the mouth of Paul's Corinthian opponents.[20] On this reading, Paul rebuts their claims by illustrating in 14:23–25 the correct way in which tongues and prophecy ought to function in the church. Johanson is adamant that there are no other possibilities:

> All other solutions . . . attributing the views of v. 22 to Paul himself are susceptible to contradictions and ambiguities, which they are unable to solve without doing

---

19. Thiselton, *First Epistle to the Corinthians*, 1122.

20. Johanson, "Tongues, a Sign for Unbelievers?," 180–203. For a modified version of Johanson's proposal see Peppiatt, *Women and Worship at Corinth*, §5.

violence to the parallelisms the literary analysis has clarified, or to the plain sense of the text itself.[21]

As much as Johanson helpfully conveys the seriousness of the conundrum, his solution is equally problematic. First, there are no internal literary markers that indicate Corinthian interjections, nor are there adversatives indicating Paul's corrective response, as there are elsewhere in the epistle (e.g., 1 Cor 6:12–17; 7:1–2; 8:1–9; 10:23–25). Second, the fact that 1 Cor 14:22 commences with the inferential ὥστε (hōste, "therefore") implies a logical continuity with what has preceded. This suggests that the meaning of 14:22 ought to be, in the first instance, a matter of harmonization with what has preceded (14:21) rather than the scene which follows (14:23–25). Curiously, the almost universal instinct of interpreters has been to identify the ἄπιστοι (apistoi) in 14:22 not with an ecclesial audience analogous to those towards whom the Isaiah prophecy is directed but with the ἄπιστοι (apistoi) in 1 Cor 14:23–25. So, Fee assumes the effect of tongues/prophecy upon unbelievers in 14:23–25 to be both the fulfillment of the Isaiah passage quoted in 14:21 and the illustration of Paul's assertion in 14:22.[22] Yet, is this necessarily so? If Paul's tongues/prophecy argument is set within an ecclesial context, and if paraphrasing Isaiah serves to progress this, then 1 Cor 14:22, which commences with ὥστε (hōte, "therefore") is almost certainly the summarizing principle of all that has preceded. Moreover, if the purpose of Isaiah's homily was to warn faithless Israel of the impending invasion of Assyria and to evoke a believing response from the people of God, the most natural reading of 1 Cor 14:22 is in these same terms: Paul is warning the Corinthians that the tongues with which they are preoccupied are a sign that they themselves are like unbelieving Israel and need to respond to Paul's prophetic word and thus become conveyors of such a prophetic ministry themselves.[23]

21. Johanson, "Tongues, a Sign for Unbelievers?," 202.

22. Fee, *First Epistle to the Corinthians*, 677, 681.

23. In Isaiah's day the speakers of tongues were the Assyrians who displaced God's people. In Corinth it is the tongue speakers who take on this foreigner-like role and bring an experience of exile to others (1 Cor 14:11, 16).

Within this interpretive framework the term σημεῖον (*sēmeion*, "sign") conveys the sense of *indication*.[24] In Isaiah's day the threat of Assyrian tongues was part of the prophetic warning to faithless Israel—tongues were indicative of divine judgment. Likewise, Corinthian tongues are not a sign of divine favor, as the "spiritual" (14:27; see 2:13, 15; 3:1) may have claimed but rather evidence of the opposite. Interestingly, Paul has already made a preparatory link in 1 Cor 14:11 where tongues result in an exilic effect in which speaker and hearer are as foreigners (βάρβαρος, *barbaros*). This consequence alludes to the covenant curses that frame Isaiah's prophecy, and reinforce that tongues, in both contexts, are indicative of God's disfavor towards his people. In this reading, the preposition εἰς (*eis*) connects tongues/prophecy with reference to the faithless/faithful rather than conveying the idea of a subjective effect directed towards particular hearers.[25] The Corinthians' childish practice of tongues is an indication not of divine favor but of disapproval—they themselves are behaving as faithless Israel.

That there are faithless insiders present within the believing community has been an important observation of the developing argument in this book. This is not to suggest that such people,

---

In Isaiah's time Assyrian tongues were a sign of impending covenant curses, that is, a warning for faithless Israel to return to the Lord and his life-giving prophetic word. In Corinth, Paul likewise seeks to warn the Corinthians in view of Israel's disobedience (see 10:1–13) and exhort them to genuine and faithful obedience. Such an ideal is characterized, as Isaiah foretold (Isa 66), by the proclamation of God's glory, which draws the gentiles alongside Israel in the worship of God.

24. BDAG, s.v. "σημεῖον." This is the normal sense in which this term is used throughout Isaiah where it is often an eschatological indication of God's salvific action, on which see Isaiah 7:14; 11:12; 13:2; 18:3; 19:20; 38:7; 55:13; 66:19.

25. In support of this reading of σημεῖον (*sēmeion*, "sign") as a divine attitude, see Collins, *First Corinthians*, 508; Carson, *Showing the Spirit*, 115. For an alternative view that the preposition εἰς (*eis*) with the accusative is for the advantage of, or conveys an effect upon, particular hearers, see Dickson, *Mission-Commitment*, 297–98; Witherington, *Conflict and Community*, 284–85; Fee, *First Epistle to the Corinthians*, 677, 680; Garland, *1 Corinthians*, 650–51; Bender, *1 Corinthians*, §14.

from the divine perspective, are "not saved" but that Paul is echoing an Old Testament prophetic tradition that exhorts the people of God to be true to their calling. Indeed, an analogous relationship between Israel and the people of God in Corinth is explicitly laid out in 1 Cor 10:1–14 where Israel's example serves as a warning to the community in Corinth: "These things happened to them as examples and were written down as warnings for us, on whom the culmination of the ages has come" (10:11; see 10:6). This typological connection further reinforces the application of the Isaiah citation in the way I have described: Paul is inviting his readers to become a people characterized not by tongues but by the presence of God's message—prophecy.

This reading of tongues as an indicative sign leads to the relatively straightforward explanation of the parallel assertion concerning prophecy in 1 Cor 14:22b. Corinthian prophecy corresponds to the Isaiah ideal of the clear and wonderful voice of the Lord (Isa 28:23–29). This prophetic word received by the redeemed community will extend to "children," and "those who are wayward in spirit will gain understanding" (Isa 29:22–24). Prophecy, then, is an indication that faithless Israel has indeed repented and that the Lord has reversed the exile and gathered his people from the places where they were scattered (Deut 30:3–4). Paul addresses those "upon whom the culmination of the ages has come" (1 Cor 10:11) and indicates that Corinthian prophecy reveals that they are no longer like faithless Israel but represent the true believing community of God's covenant people.

While the overall conclusion regarding the priority of prophecy is widely recognized in the literature, scholars admit that they are unable to discern the internal coherence of Paul's argument that leads to this conclusion.[26] Robert Nash thinks that Paul's rhetoric "simply led him a little too far in stating that prophecy was not for unbelievers."[27] Hays suggests that "Paul seems to have gotten carried away by the rhetorical antithesis of verse 22 to say something

26. Although some seem to overlook the obvious tension. See Witherington, *Conflict and Community*, 284–85.

27. Nash, *1 Corinthians*, 378.

that he does not strictly mean."[28] Fitzmyer argues that "with no little irony Paul is making the words of Isaiah refer to himself. In preaching to the Corinthians, he might just as well be speaking in tongues."[29] Bailey proposes that tongues serve in the first instance to attract outsiders to "a divine reality beyond the veil," after which their translation completes the salvific effect.[30] This reading of the dative (εἰς . . . οὐ τοῖς πιστεύουσιν ἀλλὰ τοῖς ἀπίστοις, *eis . . . ou tois pisteuousin alla tois apistois*) as one of advantage misses the wider context in which tongues are described. They are framed negatively in the Isaiah citation (14:21), in the Corinthian assembly in the final scene (14:23–25), and in the developing argument from the beginning of 1 Cor 14:1.

Thiselton is also unsure how best to explain the logic of Paul's argument, but he reaches the same overall conclusion as the one I advance:

> Christian believers should not have such a "sign" marking their community worship and thereby generating a sense of "wrongness" or "strangeness" more appropriate to what *unbelievers* might be expected to feel . . . Conversely, where prophetic speech operates with effect, this *signals* the presence and action of God in nurturing people of faith.[31]

28. Hays, *First Corinthians*, 240.

29. Fitzmyer, *First Corinthians*, 520.

30. Bailey, *Paul through Mediterranean Eyes*, 402–3. See Chrysostom, "Homilies on the Epistles of Paul 36.2," 142. Similarly, Chester mounts an argument to translate it as "you are inspired" and proposes that "tongues do serve as a sign for unbelievers, but not a sufficient one." See Chester, "Divine Madness?," 429–30. Robertson mounts a similar argument by connecting tongues with Acts 2 where they call attention to the mighty acts of God but are designed to give way to prophecy to complete the work of converting others. The key for Robertson is the background of Isaiah's signs as indicative of God's redemptive program shifting from a Jewish-centered activity to an activity involving the nations. See Robertson, "Tongues," 52–53.

31. Thiselton, *First Epistle to the Corinthians*, 1123. To solve the conundrum, Thiselton suggests a few possibilities and even considers Johanson's maxim as a resolution, on which see Thiselton, *First Epistle to the Corinthians*, 1126.

While this conclusion is consistent with Paul's overall argument, what is missing from the scholarly debate on this text is an appreciation of the way in which this sign functioned in Isaiah's context as a response-seeking warning to the covenant people. Ciampa and Rosner come closest in their identification that those confronted by Assyrian tongues were "disobedient and unbelieving Israelites."[32] Yet, they do not press further and thus also fail to apply such distinctions to the new covenant community in Corinth.[33] Despite the widely acknowledged conundrum, my relatively straightforward proposal is not, as far as I can tell, attested to in the literature. It resolves the apparent contradiction by recognizing that Paul is warning the Corinthians according to a prophetic tradition that distinguished unbelieving or faithless Israel from faithful Israel, in order to evoke from the faithless Corinthians a response of repentance.

It now remains to analyze the final verses that complete this pericope. In my view, the internal coherence of Paul's logic throughout 1 Cor 14 is maintained only when the concluding scenario (14:23–25) is understood in terms of two outsider-types who enter the Christian gathering: the ἰδιώτης (*idiōtēs*) and the (likely pagan) ἄπιστος (*apistos*). Their reaction, whether to tongues (14:23) or to prophecy (14:24–25), is a reinforcing argument that builds upon Paul's previous conclusion that prophecy ought to mark the eschatological community (14:22). Indeed, by depicting in the final scene this "idealized portrait of conversion,"[34] Paul completes his critique of the Corinthians' childishness: The

---

32. Ciampa and Rosner, *First Letter to the Corinthians*, 701.

33. Thus, Ciampa and Rosner gloss over the apparent contradiction alluding to the possibility that Paul is responding to a particular Corinthian theology of "signs." See Ciampa and Rosner, *First Letter to the Corinthians*, 702. In a later article Roy E. Ciampa offers his thinking, which "has continued to evolve." He suggests that the Isaiah background evoked by Paul serves a theological rather than historical point and thus functions quite loosely to reinforce Paul's observation of what is happening on the ground in Corinth, on which see Ciampa, "Prophecy in Corinth," 141–59.

34. Dickson, *Mission-Commitment*, 300.

outsider (now converted) recognizes what the Corinthians do not—that prophecy is indicative that God really is among his people.

Further Proof A (1 Cor 14:23) and B (1 Cor 14:24–25)

Ἐὰν οὖν συνέλθῃ ἡ ἐκκλησία ὅλη ἐπὶ τὸ αὐτὸ (A) καὶ πάντες λαλῶσιν γλώσσαις, εἰσέλθωσιν δὲ ἰδιῶται ἢ ἄπιστοι, οὐκ ἐροῦσιν ὅτι μαίνεσθε; (B) ἐὰν δὲ πάντες προφητεύωσιν, εἰσέλθῃ δέ τις ἄπιστος ἢ ἰδιώτης, ἐλέγχεται ὑπὸ πάντων, ἀνακρίνεται ὑπὸ πάντων, τὰ κρυπτὰ τῆς καρδίας αὐτοῦ φανερὰ γίνεται, καὶ οὕτως πεσὼν ἐπὶ πρόσωπον προσκυνήσει τῷ θεῷ ἀπαγγέλλων ὅτι ὄντως ὁ θεὸς ἐν ὑμῖν ἐστιν.

Ean oun synelthē hē ekklēsia holē epi to auto (A) kai pantes lalōsin glōssais, eiselthōsin de idiōtai ē apistoi, ouk erousin hoti mainesthe? (B) ean de pantes prophēteuōsin, eiselthē de tis apistos ē idiōtēs, elenchetai hypo pantōn, anakrinetai hypo pantōn, ta krypta tēs kardias autou phanera ginetai, kai houtōs pesōn epi prosōpon proskynēsei tō theō apangellōn hoti ontōs ho theos en hymin estin.

Then if the whole church gathers together and (A) everyone speaks in tongues, and the "ungifted" or unbelievers enter, will they not say: "You are out of your mind?" (B) But if everyone is prophesying and an unbeliever or "ungifted" person enters, he or she is convicted by all, judged by all—the secrets of his or her heart become known and so, falling on his or her face he or she will worship God, proclaiming, "God is truly among you!"

It is in these verses that the salvific effect of the two speech-modes become clear. So far in Paul's argument from 1 Cor 14:1, the priority of prophecy has been emphasized for its salvific effect upon believers within the community: "The one who prophesies speaks to people for their strengthening, encouraging and comfort" (14:3). This motif of an intra-ecclesial love ethic was evident throughout 1 Cor 8–10 and continues through the subsequent section by means of the body metaphor (11:29; 12:7, 25; 14:3–4). Now, however, Paul extends his tongues/prophecy contrast to invite a consideration of their respective effects upon the two types of outsiders who may be present: the ἰδιῶται (*idiōtai*) and the ἄπιστοι (*apistoi*, 14:23–25).

Scholars differ over whether these terms are synonymous or even supplement one another (e.g., "unbelieving novices"),[35] or indeed, as I will argue, whether Paul intends to speak about two distinct types of people. The reversal of the order of the "couplet" between 1 Cor 14:23 and 14:24 suggests a rhetorical intentionality on Paul's part. Dickson argues that in 14:23, due to the "effect" of tongues, the uninformed person is revealed as an unbeliever, while in 14:24–25 the order is reversed and the apparent unbelieving person turns out to be only uninformed, showing themselves to be among those who would believe.[36] This is Dickson's attempt at correlating Paul's use of these identity descriptors with the way in which he understands 14:22 to outline the effect of tongues/prophecy upon unbelievers/believers. Yet the particle ἤ (*ē*, "or") distinguishes between two distinct types of outsiders, both of whom are readily distinguishable from those insiders whom Paul addresses in 1 Cor 14:22. Again, I contend that 14:22 conveys Paul's concluding principles of the intra-ecclesial tongues/prophecy section, and thus 14:23–25 represents a distinct but reinforcing proof for what has gone before. Whereas the οὖν (*oun*) commencing 14:23 is widely translated as an inferential (e.g. "therefore"), its place within a condition clause, Ἐὰν οὖν . . . (*Ean oun*), is better understood to convey a transitional function (e.g., "now, then"; see 1 Cor 6:4; 14:11). That 1 Cor 14:23–25 is not the climactic summary to which Paul is moving is further supported by the abrupt return to internal matters from 14:26. It is my contention that the internal coherence of Paul's argument, along with his rhetorical emphasis, is best explained when 1 Cor 14:23–25 is understood

---

35. Kistemaker, *Exposition*, 502. Those who prefer synonyms include Garland, *1 Corinthians*, 651; Hays, *First Corinthians*, 238; Fee, *First Epistle to the Corinthians*, 685.

36. Dickson, *Mission-Commitment*, 298–99.

not as the illustration of Paul's assertion in 14:22 but as a reinforcing argument of an already stated conclusion.

In the first scenario (14:23), Paul conveys the effect of tongues on outsiders, with a particular but not exclusive emphasis upon the ἰδιώτης (*idiotēs*, "an 'ungifted' person"). By placing this first in the couplet, Paul calls to mind the previous effect of alienation that this outsider-type has experienced (14:11, 16). This time, however, the effect is not simply an inability to participate, but an overt aversion expressed by the rhetorical question, "Will they not say: 'You are out of your mind?'" (14:23), which some interpreters associate with the ecstatic frenzy in contemporaneous mystery religions.[37] However, it is reasonable to assume that Paul is being less specific and simply exaggerating for effect, reinforcing the confusion that can arise from an experience that is unintelligible (14:9), alienating (14:11), and exclusive (14:16).[38] His point, in the words of Perkins, is clear enough: "Uncontrolled speaking in tongues actually hinders the mission of the community."[39] There is no apparent contradiction with what Paul has previously stated in 1 Cor 14:22. Once again, Assyrian tongues in Isaiah's judgment oracle serve to reinforce Paul's assertion that Corinthian tongues are likewise a warning to faithless insiders within the community. That the outsider is alienated through such an experience further reinforces that such a speech-mode, at least in the assembly, does not reflect the presence or purpose of God, and therefore is detrimental, as far as the salvific welfare of others is concerned.

Whereas tongues serve neither the salvific welfare of the insider (14:1–22) nor the outsider (14:23), prophecy can result in salvific benefit—first to one's fellow believer (14:1–22) and, now, Paul will argue, to outsiders (14:24–25). The ἄπιστος (*apistos*, "an

37. "Ecstatic" and "rave" speech-modes are mentioned in the extant literature, on which see Malcolm, *World of 1 Corinthians*, 129. See Hays, *First Corinthians*, 238; Fee, *First Epistle to the Corinthians*, 685; and Perkins, *First Corinthians*, 162.

38. The meaning of μαίνομαι (*mainomai*, "to be out of one's mind") elsewhere in the New Testament carries this more generic sense. See John 10:20; Acts 12:25; 26:24–25.

39. Perkins, *First Corinthians*, 161.

unbeliever") now appears first, signifying that this type of outsider most fittingly corresponds with an experience of conversion. Yet, in the eyes of at least some in the church, the ἰδιώτης (*idiotēs*, "an 'ungifted' person") also needs conversion, so for persuasive purposes, Paul also includes them. The depiction of these outsiders' conversion involves two aspects. First, the gathered insiders are themselves agents of the conversion: the outsider is "convicted by all, judged by all" (14:24). The verb ἀνακρίνω (*anakrinō*, "to judge"), occurring also in 1 Cor 2:15, depicts an activity of the ideal spiritual person. Whereas the Corinthians thought that tongues were indicative of their spiritual status, Paul contradicts this by aligning the act of judgment with the truly spiritual activity of prophecy. The second aspect of this scenario is the effect upon the outsider: "falling on his or her face he or she will worship God" (14:25). Dickson portrays this as an "idealized portrait of conversion, styled on the great 'conversions' described in the Jewish Scriptures."[40] This is a sobering explanation of the posture of the truly spiritual, which contrasts sharply with the inflated ego of the Corinthians (4:6, 18–19; 5:2; 8:1; see 13:4). Ironically, the new convert recognizes what the Corinthians failed to understand: that "God is truly among you!" (14:25). This response echoes Zech 8:23 and importantly Isa 45:14 (see Isa 49:23; 60:20–36) in which the post-exilic restoration of God's people is recognized as evidence of God's presence, even by the nations.[41] Tucker notes the "striking" use of the out-group to influence those within the Christ-group: "Even outsiders will see God is with their Christ-group."[42]

The presence of God among his people brings the temple theme, so prevalent throughout 1 Corinthians, to its climax. The prophetic ministry of the Corinthians does not simply signal divine approval but serves as evidence that they indeed are

---

40. Dickson cites occurrences in the LXX of the phrase πεσὼν ἐπὶ πρόσωπον (*pesōn epi prosōpon*) in Gen 17:3; Lev 9:24; Num 16:22; Ezek 11:13. See Dickson, *Mission-Commitment*, 300.

41. Ciampa and Rosner, *First Letter to the Corinthians*, 706–7; Hays, *First Corinthians*, 239.

42. Tucker, "1 Corinthians," 319.

the eschatological community through which the nations will be drawn to glorify God. No longer are they simply beneficiaries of Isaiah's prophecy but servants who bring salvific benefits to the nations. The rhetorical effect of this scene upon Paul's readers is palpable. While tongues correspond with exile, prophecy indicates both an experience of God's vertical salvation and a horizontal participation in the priestly vocation of promoting God's reputation among the nations.

In this detailed exegetical analysis of 1 Cor 14:20–25, I have sought to outline the internal coherence of Paul's argument while accounting for the pertinent sociorhetorical features of the text. It remains to consider the socioreligious nature of the Corinthian gatherings and the extent to which such assemblies may have been oriented towards outsiders.

THE SOCIORELIGIOUS NATURE OF CORINTHIAN GATHERINGS

The salvific potential of the gathering described in 1 Cor 14:23–25 invites further consideration of its nature and how outsiders are present. References to Corinthian assemblies occur first in 1 Cor 5:4 (συνάγω, *synagō*, "to assemble") and regularly throughout 1 Cor 11 and 14 (συνέρχομαι, *synerchomai*, "to come together," 11:17–18, 20, 33–34; 14:23, 26). These occurrences, along with the evidence in the wider literary context, provide a picture of the Corinthian community (or at least Paul's expectations of it) eating together (including the Lord's Supper), praying, prophesying, teaching, psalm singing, exercising gifts, expressing care for one another, and even acting to exclude the immoral insider. At least some of these practices reflect a familiarity with the liturgical pattern of synagogue worship.[43] As with most Pauline communities, the founding members of the Corinthian church were likely to have been Jewish, thereby incorporating such patterns into their

---

43. McKnight, *Light among the Gentiles*, 62; Martin, *Worship in the Early Church*, 19. Col 3:15–17 may indicate similar aspects of early Christian gatherings. A further non-Pauline account is found in Acts 2:42–47.

new beliefs and developing religious practices. Such a connection may explain, in part, the openness to outsiders that is assumed in 1 Cor 14:23–25. Literary evidence from the period attests to Jewish awareness that their religious activities may hold missiological implications for gentile observers. So, Philo imagines the synagogue standing "wide open" in every city,[44] and Josephus comments on "multitudes of Greeks" in Antioch whom the Jews were "attracting to their religious ceremonies."[45] While such texts cannot bear the full weight of a developed missiological ideal within first-century Judaism, they certainly indicate the possibility that formal synagogue services may have had an influence upon wider ethnic groups. Arguably, a similar awareness may have shaped the early Jewish membership of the church in Corinth, thereby giving some missional shape to these early gatherings of believers.

What the Corinthians did not have, however, was an equivalent building to a synagogue in which to gather. Murphy-O'Connor's influential article "House-Churches and the Eucharist" continues to be upheld as a credible explanation of a house-based community in Corinth.[46] By imagining a gathering of the whole church (1 Cor 14:23) in the home of a wealthy villa owner, Murphy-O'Connor draws from archaeological evidence of floor space to propose a total membership of fifty people and an explanation of why such a gathering of the whole church was the exception

44. Philo, *Spec. Laws* 2:62. While such statements by no means convey a missiological intent behind the synagogue, they do provide some evidence of Jewish awareness as to the power and attractiveness of their religious activities, including the place of the synagogue, in drawing in gentiles. Dickson argues that such texts express a rich Old Testament tradition where "the gathered faithful . . . conduct their public worship in full 'hearing' of the Gentiles among whom they live." He quotes Ps 96:1–3: "O sing to the Lord a new song . . . Declare his glory among the nations, his marvelous works among all peoples." See Dickson, *Mission-Commitment*, 74, 77, 79. McKnight is more circumspect: "I do not doubt that Gentiles . . . may have eventually come to convert through synagogue expositions. However . . . it seems to me that it was almost predominantly for the instruction of the Jews." See McKnight, *Light among the Gentile*, 65–66.

45. Josephus, *J.W.* 7:43–45.

46. Murphy-O'Connor, *Keys to First Corinthians.*

rather than the rule.[47] There are, however, more recent criticisms of Murphy-O'Connor's assumptions. Horrell describes an equally "imaginative" possibility, pointing to the East Theatre Street excavations as an alternative domestic space with significantly more capacity for larger catered gatherings.[48] The key word is "imaginative"—archaeological evidence is limited, and any attempt to reconstruct the Corinthian gatherings through such means requires a series of vulnerable assumptions.

In this debate, which is largely speculative, scholars are trying to reconstruct the type of venue in which such gatherings took place and the demography of the early Corinthian community, both in terms of size and social status. John Kloppenborg is suspicious of such "critical space theory" and instead suggests that data from comparable Greco-Roman cultic associations and occupational guilds provides a better model of membership numbers and venue use. On this basis, he proposes a total membership of fifteen to thirty people who probably used a range of spaces, including non-domestic settings.[49] Yet such a low number seems unlikely given the extent and complexity of the social, moral, and theological matters which Paul addresses in 1 Corinthians. Indeed, a report from Chloe's household leads to Paul referencing four personality-based identity groups after which three further persons are mentioned (1 Cor 1:11–17). The scholarly consensus is considerably higher, with around fourteen male members identified in the Corinthian correspondence. Where such members represented a household, they may have contained further family members and even slaves who were incorporated into church membership. While the range of membership possibilities proposed by scholars are as low as fifteen and as high as two hundred, an estimation even somewhere in between conveys the social reality of a relatively small association of Christ-followers in a city estimated to have had forty to fifty thousand residents.[50]

---

47. Murphy-O'Connor, *Keys to First Corinthians*, 182–86.

48. Horrell, *Making of Christian Morality*, 38–48.

49. Kloppenborg, *Christ's Associations*, 97, 105–6.

50. Murphy-O'Connor counts fourteen male members in Corinth from

Aspects of this discussion bear upon how outsiders may have been present at such gatherings. Kloppenborg, for example, reviews five possible venues and their implications for how an outsider (whom he describes as a visitor, uninvited guest, curious passer-by) could have entered the Christian gathering.[51] However, such outsider characterizations impose an imagined social situation that is incongruent with the text itself. Chambers, too, makes this same error when he describes an "accidental visitor" who happens to wander in en route to the shops.[52] Yet, in the prior literary analysis, at least one outsider-type mentioned in the text, the ἰδιώτης (*idiōtēs*, "an 'ungifted' person," 14:23–35), is not a visitor to the meeting but already inside it (14:11, 16).[53] This leaves only the possibility that the other outsider-type, the ἄπιστος (*apistos*, "an unbeliever") might fit such an "accidental" or "uninvited" description.

The term ἄπιστος (*apistos*, "unbeliever") occurs with relative frequency throughout 1 Corinthians to describe unbelievers who are distinct from the believing community. They are the unrighteous before whom the Corinthians appear for court cases (6:6), they are those to whom believers may be married (7:12–16), and they are dining hosts into whose homes the Christian has been

---

Paul's letters and estimates a total membership of fifty, on which see Murphy-O'Connor, *Keys to First Corinthians*, 183. Barnett infers from the text that there may have been more than fifteen household groups (each with between twelve to fifteen members, giving an upper total possibility of two hundred) that made up the churches in Corinth, on which see Barnett, *Corinthian Question*, 225–27. Willet draws from a range of methodologies to posit a city population of thirty to fifty thousand with an additional rural population of approximately ten thousand. See Willet, "Whirlwind of Numbers," 127–58.

51. Kloppenborg, *Christ's Associations*, 118–20.

52. This social reconstruction forms part of Chambers' explanation that in 1 Cor 14:23–25 Paul is concerned with the avoidance of negative outcomes rather than the conversion of unbelievers, on which see Chambers, "Paul, His Converts," 211–12.

53. Even if a broader definition of an ἰδιώτης (*idiōtēs*) is adopted, such as Andrew Clarke's "somebody who is in the process of gaining fuller incorporation," the non-accidental nature of their attendance is clear. See Clarke, "Church Membership and the ἰδιώτης," 207.

invited (10:27). It is for these reasons that Kevin Munoz refers to such outsiders as "insiders in the most socially serious ways."[54] If Paul assumes the believing community is to maintain significant social engagement with their wider community (1 Cor 5:9–13), then the unbelieving outsider who is present in the gathering is almost certainly someone socially connected to them rather than an accidental visitor.

That this is the case is supported by the essentially social nature of Corinthian gatherings. Perhaps reflecting Greco-Roman dining culture, 1 Cor 11:17–33 assumes a comprehensive meal experience. Although 1 Cor 14:23 references the whole church gathering in a formal way, the implication is that such was not the only form of assembling. There were presumably many other less formal and highly social gatherings in which the principle of 1 Cor 14:23–25 may have applied, namely, that outsiders might be present at their Christian gatherings, especially where the venue was a domestic context.[55] It is not difficult to imagine who such people may have been. The Corinthian community was a very small association whose members would necessarily have been embedded in diverse social networks—friends, neighbors, family, coworkers, business associates, patrons, and clients.[56] Paul is outlining an ecclesial vision which conveys a salvific effect upon the ἄπιστος (*apistos*, "unbeliever") *among them*. Indeed, Paul's point in 1 Cor 14:23–25 is not that they are unexpected but that the expectation of their presence should shape the practice of their meeting. Dickson points out that the effectiveness of Paul's argument rests upon this shared assumption that such people were indeed present and their conversion desirable:

> That Paul speaks of the presence of outsiders at public worship suggests that the scenario was not (as far as he was concerned) out of the ordinary. The argument would lack substance entirely were the "hypotheticals" not believable in the minds of Paul's readers . . . Paul clearly

54. Munoz, "How Not to Go Out," 985.

55. Clarke, "Church Membership and the ἰδιώτης," 205.

56. Munoz, "How Not to Go Out," 115.

> believed that the visitor's presence at public worship contained mission possibilities.[57]

Such a reconstruction of the social setting and shared assumptions of Paul and his readers invites a further consideration of the extent to which Paul intended such outsiders to be the direct beneficiaries of prophecy in the assembly.

PROPHECY AND THE OUTSIDER

Given these shared missional assumptions about outsiders who may be present in Corinthian gatherings, to what extent did Paul's ecclesial vision assume that such people were the intentional object of the prophetic ministry that the congregation was exercising? Curiously, scholars are reluctant to identify the prophetic ministry described in 1 Cor 14:24–25 as one which is directed towards the outsiders who may be present. So, Dickson, despite an insistence that "public worship contained mission possibilities," states, "This is not to say the prophetic speech of v. 24 is in any way directed towards the outsider . . . he merely 'overhears' a typical utterance aimed at the gathered faithful."[58] Don Carson, too, stresses that the unbeliever "comes in and overhears what is going on in the assembly."[59] Such claims rightly identify the intra-ecclesial context of Paul's wider tongues/prophecy discourse. Paul is, in the first instance, developing an argument for the superiority of prophecy because it corresponds most directly with an ethic of love (14:1) and serves as an intelligible speech-mode (14:9) directed towards the edification, encouragement, and comfort of others (14:3). Yet, there are three reasons why this prophetic speech-mode also includes a more direct salvific intention towards outsiders.

57. Dickson, *Mission-Commitment*, 299–300.

58. Dickson, *Mission-Commitment*, 300–301. For Dickson, speech as a verbal apologetic corresponds more properly with the daily conversations of converts with outsiders, on which see *Mission-Commitment*, 302.

59. Carson, *Showing the Spirit*, 116.

First, the social profile of the Corinthian assembly suggests that, at least in the case of the ἰδιώτης (*idiōtēs*, "'ungifted' person"), some of the outsiders mentioned in 1 Cor 14:23–25 were within the assembly. Once again, Paul's criticism of tongues was due to their alienating effect upon such "inside outsiders" (14:11, 16)—the clear implication being that such people ought to be the recipients of a prophetic speech-mode, the aim of which is to build them up. Given the way in which Paul places the ungifted and unbeliever together as a couplet (14:23–25), it is reasonable to assume that Paul would equally have considered the ἄπιστος (*apistos*, "unbeliever") as an appropriate object of the Corinthians' prophetic ministry.

Secondly, given that the ἄπιστοι (*apistoi*, "unbelievers") were significantly socially associated with the believing community, it would be strange to think that they would merely overhear what is said. Prophecy was inherently a speech-mode ordered for the salvific welfare of others and quite probably was directed towards *all* those who were present, including those whom the community would be eager to see converted.

Finally, whereas scholars tend to frame their analysis in terms of the mission possibilities of "public worship," such a term is somewhat anachronistic. These gatherings, as outlined previously, were both formal and informal socioreligious occasions in which various aspects of what might be considered "worship" featured. Yet, they were not worship services in the way that a modern reader might imagine. Within the socially flexible contexts in which the Corinthians assembled, it is possible to imagine speech-modes functioning that were deliberately engaging with outsiders who were present. Indeed, efforts to engage directly with unbelieving family members, friends, and associates would certainly be consistent with the missiological implications of their eschatological temple identity that Paul has been nurturing throughout the epistle.

CONCLUSION

In this chapter I have argued for the internal coherence of Paul's argument in 1 Cor 14:20–25. Whereas most interpreters seek to harmonize the reaction of the outsiders (14:23–25) with Paul's assertions in 14:22, I have proposed that the paraphrase of Isa 28:11–12 establishes an intra-ecclesial distinction between faithless and faithful Israel, which Paul then applies to the Corinthian assembly in terms of two principles: (1) tongues, in the gathered community and untranslated, are an indication of faithless Corinth, while (2) prophecy is the sign of God's favor towards faithful Corinth. The rhetoric serves, as it did in Isaiah's day, as response-seeking—Paul is exhorting his readers to the sort of maturity that values prophecy: the indication of God's presence among and through them. Given that I have argued that Paul summarizes his argument in 1 Cor 14:22, this means that the subsequent scenario, which depicts outsider reactions to tongues and prophecy, is a reinforcing point rather than the climactic one. This reading, to the best of my knowledge, is unique, and it offers a promising resolution to the interpretive difficulties which have plagued this text. Importantly, the developing temple motif also reaches its climax through the conversion of the pagan. Paul has identified the ministry of the prophesying church as analogous to the restoration of Israel and her temple, through which the priestly and prophetic role of Israel is now to be realized in Corinth as their own prophetic activity connects the gentiles to Yahweh (Isa 41:8–10; 42:6; 43:10, 12; 44:8; 61:1–3; 66:19; Exod 19:4–6).

The extent to which prophecy is directed towards, or merely overheard by, outsiders is an underdeveloped discussion in the literature. Even among those who propose the "public worship" of the gathered community as containing missional possibilities, there is reluctance to identify a direct and intentional orientation towards outsiders. Yet, analysis of the social profile of the Corinthian community casts new light upon such assumptions: insider identity in Corinth is complex, and there may be some within the community who are merely so-called brothers towards whom salvific intention is appropriate. Moreover, the outsider groups are hardly accidental visitors or curious passers-by as some have imagined them. The ἰδιώτης (*idiōtēs*, "'ungifted' person") finds reference in the wider text as present within the assembly and one whom Paul laments as alienated by Corinthian tongues. Likewise, the ἄπιστοι (*apistoi*, "unbelievers"), when considered in the context of the entire letter, are insiders in a social sense—highly connected through household and social networks. Additionally, rather than imagining "public worship" as an event, the social nature of Corinthian gatherings, in various household settings and with varying degrees of formality, suggests that speech-modes directed towards the salvific welfare of outsiders would have occurred. After all, prophecy was intended to build up the community of faith, and this involved the inclusion of more "Greeks" and "Jews" into the "church of God."

Conclusion

An Authentic Missional Identity—Then and Now

WHEN PAUL PENNED 1 CORINTHIANS he wrote to a community that he had founded only five years earlier. Indeed, many in the church were more recent converts and some from a pagan rather than Jewish background. The evidence suggests a troubled community—socially, morally, and theologically. Not only was it young, but it was also relatively small. If there were just one hundred believers to whom Paul wrote, in a city of approximately fifty thousand residents, these Christians would have made up just 0.2 percent of the population of mid-first-century Roman Corinth.[1] No wonder Paul responds to the idea of dissociation from the immoral and idolaters in an emphatic manner: "Not at all . . . In that case you would have to leave this world" (1 Cor 5:10). As a relatively small religious association, believers found themselves in households and wider social and political networks in which they were likely the only Christ-followers. This background may explain, in part, why a straightforward missionary commissioning of the Corinthians would have, from Paul's perspective, assumed too much. Instead, he aimed first to engender in them an ecclesial identity that would foster the social, moral, and theological reform so necessary for them, and that would fuel an authentic Christian confidence. By recognizing this approach as Paul's own,

1. See Willet, "Whirlwind of Numbers," 127–58. The estimate of one hundred Christians is based on an in-between evaluation offered by scholars; see chapter 4 of this book.

the interpreter will be alert to the way in which this new ecclesial identity is inherently missional, giving rise to consistent expectations for the Corinthians to adopt a posture of salvific intentionality both within their community and towards unbelievers. In the following sections, I will draw together the findings of this study, connecting them with an emerging missional hermeneutical discussion, and then apply them to contemporary ecclesial mission practice.

AN UNTIDY MISSIONAL IDENTITY

An important part of appreciating this missional identity lies in recognizing the untidy sociotheological profile of the Corinthians themselves. That 1 Corinthians contains such significant social, moral, and theological instruction reveals the extent to which these young insiders were still coming to terms with their own authentic Christian identity.[2] Paul's consistent reminder to them of their status *in Christ* (1 Cor 1:2, 30; 3:23; 6:11–15; 10:16; 12:12, 27; 15:22) does not simply recall their salvation experience but commits them also to a set of intra-ecclesial relationships characterized by a common concern for each other's salvific welfare. Hence, the immoral man is to be excluded for his salvific good, as well as for that of the entire community (5:1–8), and the Corinthians are to build up one another and avoid any idolatrous scenario in which they may imperil the salvation of a fellow believer (8:1–13). An important way in which Paul reinforces these salvific obligations is by casting their ecclesial identity as an alternative temple community in the tradition of the Old Testament (3:16–17; 6:18–20; 10:14–22, 31; 14:25). Such imagery lends itself to a critique of immorality and idolatry in a way that emphasizes that they belong to God (6:19; 10:14, 31), and that each has the salvific responsibility to build one another up towards this reality (14:1–22).

This temple imagery also frames a series of relationships with outsiders that contain salvific possibilities. So, the believer in

2. Lang, "Trouble with Insiders," 981–82.

a mixed marriage is given a theological vision of their sanctifying influence, which may result in the salvation of their spouse (7:12–16). Likewise, Paul exhorts the believer to refrain from idol-food when as a guest of a pagan host, appealing to their obligation to seek the salvific welfare of others and to glorify God (10:23–33). Moreover, in 1 Cor 14:23–25, an explicit missional identity reinforces the priority of prophecy as the normative speech-mode of the gathered community. Indeed, it is through such prophecy that the Corinthians are identified as the eschatological temple community through whom the gentiles will come to worship the Lord. As insider theological identity has been noted to be untidy, so too has outsider identity. A key observation throughout this study is that these theological outsiders are, at times, revealed to be insiders, at least in a social sense. They are married to believers, dine with them, and exist in a range of inevitable social networks with them, some of which may explain why unbelievers are even present at specifically Christian assemblies.

In addition to this salvific network of insider and outsider relationships in which the Corinthians live, the apostle Paul himself also provides a vital reference point for their missional identity. While this study has quite deliberately undertaken a literary and sociorhetorical approach from below, concentrating on Paul's expectations upon his readers, such are deliberately framed in 1 Cor 11:1 as an imitation of Paul himself. Paul's own apostolic task is expressed in 1 Cor 9:19–23 in which his missional undertakings to both Jews and gentiles are framed as a participation in the gospel. It is this same goal that is to characterize the Corinthians as they imitate Paul and partner in the saving effect of the gospel (10:31—11:1). Paul's extension of this imitation ideal back to Christ himself both reinforces their ecclesial missional identity as well as clarifies an important distinction between Christ, Paul, and the Corinthians. The apostleship of Paul is an expression of Christ's mission but not the same as it—his rhetorical question, "Was Paul crucified for you?" (1 Cor 1:13), says as much. As the expression of Paul's mission differs from Christ's, so too the Corinthians' mission, while founded in Christ, is expressed differently from that of both Christ and Paul. Johannes Nissen helpfully differentiates between *mission* and *missions*:

> The first refers primarily to the *missio Dei* (God's mission), that is, God's self-revelation as the One who loves the world, God's involvement in and with the world. *Missions (the missiones ecclesiae*: the missionary venture of the church) refers to particular forms, related to specific times, places, or needs, of participation in *missio Dei [sic]*.[3]

This conceptual language is an important part of answering the great omission with which this book began. Rather than accept Bowers's distinction of missionary activity in terms of Paul's active evangelism and the church's passive role of supportive partnership, Nissen's "missionary venture of the church" invites an investigation of the text that accounts for Paul's expectations of the Corinthians' mission as one which is in continuity with Christ's. Indeed, through a series of scenarios that capture the very real situations in which his readers would have found themselves, Paul cultivates within them a missional imagination that he expected would express itself through both ethical distinctives and verbal explanations consistent with their faith commitment. This might be described as promoting a comprehensive and integrated missional identity that was distinct and appropriate for their ecclesial and social circumstances, and that Paul grounded in a common mission based in Christ's own—the *missio Dei*. This summation relates to important features of an emerging field of inquiry called *missional hermeneutics*.

---

3. Nissen, *New Testament and Mission*, 17. See O'Brien, *Consumed by Passion*, 106–7; Barram, *Mission and Moral Reflection*, 42–77; Barram, "Pauline Mission as Salvific Intentionality," 235–41.

FIRST CORINTHIANS AND MISSIONAL HERMENEUTICS

Aspects of this study have touched upon an ongoing dialogue between Pauline exegetes and scholars of mission as to the framing of the New Testament in terms of the *missio Dei*. In my view, this study of Paul's ecclesial missiology in action within 1 Corinthians contributes to the emerging missional hermeneutic conversation. In 2011, George Hunsberger mapped out four of its "streams of emphasis" and applied them to biblical interpretation: (1) the missional direction of the story; (2) the missional purposes of the writings; (3) the missional locatedness of the readers; and (4) missional engagement with cultures.[4] In what follows, I briefly highlight where my exegetical study complements this hermeneutical movement.

The Missional Direction of the Story

The structure and content of Paul's thought, evident throughout 1 Corinthians, corresponds to the wider framework of the *missio Dei*. In an extended introduction, the Christ event is anchored in a series of citations from Isaiah (1 Cor 1:17—2:16). The cosmic and eschatological nature of this salvific event is further confirmed in 1 Cor 15 in which the resurrection of the Christ reverses the decay inherent in Adam. The stories and traditions of Israel feature throughout the epistle as indicators and warnings for the Corinthian community who now experience the fulfillment of the ages (10:1–13; see 5:7–8, 13; 6:16; 9:9; 11:23–26; 14:21; 15:12–34). It is apparent that Paul does not simply see a fundamental unity in the structure of salvation history but that he also considers himself as an eschatological herald of this gospel that has been entrusted to him (1:17; 9:17). This missionary activity he traces back to Christ

---

4. Hunsberger, "Proposals for a Missional Hermeneutic," 309–21. See the summary in Gorman, *Becoming the Gospel*, 50–62. Given that Hunsberger himself acknowledges that the fourth stream is an extension of the second, I will restrict my analysis to the first three streams.

himself (11:1), the missionary par excellence, whose death and resurrection inaugurates this new salvific era. Significantly, Paul considers himself a participant in the salvific effects of the gospel (9:23) and an expert builder who laid the foundations of what the Corinthians are becoming (3:5). This reference to building gives way to the emerging motif of temple from 1 Cor 3:16 (see 6:19; 7:14; 10:21, 31; 14:25) with which Paul will foster an ecclesial identity that participates in the missional direction that the prophets foreshadowed at the end of the age: that "people of all languages and nations will take firm hold of one Jew . . . and say, 'Let us go with you, because we have heard that God is with you'" (Zech 8:23; see 1 Cor 14:25).

The Missional Purposes of Paul's Writings

This inherent missional structure to Paul's thought, along with his self-understanding, also holds important implications for the missional purposes of his writings. The occasional nature of 1 Corinthians is well recognized from the range of matters addressed, many of the details of which are opaque to the contemporary interpreter. Yet, as has been noted throughout this book, Paul does not simply address mere social or moral or even theological concerns, but he seeks to cultivate a new ecclesial identity with inherent missional implications. By analyzing salvific language and concepts, this study has outlined the way in which Paul expected his readers to adopt a posture of horizontal salvific intentionality towards those within the church and outsiders with whom they were socially connected. Whereas missional hermeneutics has emerged, in part, as a response to the apparent absence of an ecclesial missionary mandate in Paul's letters, the language of salvific intentionality within 1 Corinthians suggests that a missional reading of this epistle is not a mere matter of inference but integral to Paul's purposes in writing.

The Missional Locatedness of Today's Readers

An important third stream of Hunsberger's mapping of missional hermeneutics is the way in which faithful interpretation invites the reading community to understand their own locatedness within the mission into which the text summons them to participate. To draw from 1 Cor 10:11, the challenge is how the church of today also stands in the overlap of the ages and thus is that upon whom the fulfillment of the ages has come. The historical hermeneutics that have featured throughout this study ought not to construe the "past" as meaning "alien."[5] As Oliver O'Donovan points out, "cultural foreignness . . . is not a final barrier to understanding, but a warning against shallow understanding."[6] Notably, the purpose of this study has been to deepen understanding, by first locating the *missio Dei* in action in first-century Corinth and then to commence Hunsberger's "conversation between former times and places and current ones."[7]

Whereas Hunsberger's initial two streams are predicated on a biblical-theological explanation of inherent structures of missional thought within Scripture itself, this third stream, which locates the contemporary reader in this missional story, first requires the hermeneutical approaches that have featured throughout this book. Wayne Meeks notes that "texts do not carry their meaning within themselves, but 'mean' insofar as they function intelligibly within specific cultures or subcultures."[8] This study of 1 Corinthians has sought, within the constraints of the evidence available, to understand such *meaning* for those first believers in the various horizontal salvific scenarios that Paul outlines throughout the epistle. Through such approaches, the contemporary interpreter is not alienated from the past but brought nearer to it. The tools

---

5. O'Donovan, *Resurrection and Moral Order*, 161.

6. O'Donovan, *Resurrection and Moral Order*, 161.

7. Hunsberger, "Proposals for a Missional Hermeneutic," 316. See also the "two-way missional exegesis" from "God's Word to human context" and vice versa in van Aarde and li-M, "Fruitful Missional Exegesis," 6–9.

8. Meeks, "Hermeneutics of Social Embodiment," 192.

of rhetorical analysis and sociohistorical inquiry offer clarity to the meaning of the text and invite a cultivation of what Hays calls "imaginative acts":

> The use of the New Testament in normative ethics requires an *integrative act of the imagination,* a discernment about how our lives, despite their historical dissimilarities to the lives narrated in the New Testament, might fitly answer to that narration and participate in the truth that it tells.[9]

In the case of 1 Corinthians this requires careful analysis of the social features of the Corinthian community, its recent formation and minority status, its complex sociotheological profile, and the challenges and opportunities it faced. Through imagining their social vulnerability, their moral and theological immaturity, the vulnerability of a believing wife with a pagan spouse, the high social cost of self-exclusion from idolatry, and the significant level of association they had with unbelievers, the contemporary church can begin to imagine itself as a missional community in its own complex social setting. This imagining takes place through an epistemological shift whereby the church reads Scripture through "eyes of faith" as it takes up its place in the *missio Dei.*[10]

A MISSIONARY ENCOUNTER WITH THE WEST

In what ways ought we, as today's readers, to embody the missional truths narrated in 1 Corinthians, locating ourselves as participants in the *missio Dei*? In recent decades there has been renewed interest in what Lesslie Newbigin describes as a genuinely missionary encounter between the gospel and modern Western culture.[11] Whereas in the not-so-distant past Western society and Christian

---

9. Hays, *Moral Vision,* 298. Consider also O'Donovan, who describes ethical thinking in terms of carefully correlating the "moral thought" within the text with the situation "presented by our own pastoral situations." See O'Donovan, *Self, World, and Time,* 78–80.

10. McKinzie, "Missional Hermeneutics," 177.

11. Newbigin, *Foolishness to the Greeks,* 3.

identity were closely aligned, missiologists now universally describe the social context of the Western church as post-Christian. Yet, there is little to indicate that the church itself has come to terms with what have been rapid and remarkable changes. Missiologist Michael Frost points out that "although the Christendom story no longer defines Western culture in general, it remains the primary definer of the church's self-understanding in almost every Western nation."[12] Frost argues that a new meta-narrative is needed—one from which fresh missional postures can emerge. Yet, for Newbigin, the reason for such a missionary encounter is not simply because the West has changed but because the church itself has capitulated to the prevailing ideological trends of culture.[13] In other words, missional locatedness is not simply a matter of adaptation to a changing cultural setting but of being present within that context in a way that fittingly corresponds to the identity, missional and otherwise, that Christ has *already given*. In this penultimate section I briefly map the way in which a Corinthian missiology in action might correspond to a contemporary missional identity and practice. In conversation with Lesslie Newbigin, David Bosch, and Miroslav Volf, I outline a missional identity already given in Christ—one that is corporate rather than simply individual, one in which ecclesial boundaries are soft rather than hard, one that disseminates rather than centralizes salvific agency, and one that manifests Christian faith rather than simply proclaims it.

A Corporate Missional Identity

In the introductory chapter of this book I noted that traditional approaches within missional scholarship tend to identify the apostle Paul as the paradigm for missiology. As a result, verbal modes of mission-commitment become the primary way in which mission is conceptualized. Consequently, the historical debate has

12. Frost, *Exiles*, 5.

13. Newbigin, "England as a Foreign Mission Field," 2. For a summary of Newbigin's critique of the syncretism within Western Christianity see Goheen, *Church and Its Vocation*, 166–68.

become hermeneutically fixed within categories of active (verbal) and passive (supporting) expressions of mission-commitment, with scholarship divided as to the form most properly corresponding to the mission of the church in the New Testament. Another consequence of this perspective is that mission-commitment is overly individualized. Paul, of course, writes as an individual (or at least as part of a small team) and as an apostle, and the direct appropriation of his missionary consciousness and activities to the ecclesial community results in an understandable emphasis on individual verbal expressions of mission. While the imitation ideal of salvific intentionality emerges from a common mission founded in Christ and shared with Paul (1 Cor 11:1), I have argued there remain important distinctions between Christ, the apostle, and the ecclesial community. These differences have been discerned by the adoption of an alternative method apparent throughout this book: a missiology from below.

Approaching a missiological investigation of 1 Corinthians from below privileges the way in which Paul's readers understood and expressed the expectations which the apostle laid upon them. This method, to borrow from Hunsberger's third stream of missional hermeneutics, reads the text from the perspective of the missional situation of the Corinthians. The result is not simply a widening of examples of the way in which Paul invited them to express salvific intentionality but also a fresh appreciation of the way in which Paul cultivates the *missional identity* of the ecclesial community. Identity, which refers to the personal and social aspects of self-concept, is an important and emerging area of scholarly interest in the Corinthian correspondence.[14] Whereas modern Western culture is widely recognized for its developed conception

14. See Brian Tucker's overview of social identity approaches in Tucker, *Reading 1 Corinthians*, §1–2. See Lim, *Metaphors and Social Identity*, §2. Charles Taylor offers a "spatial metaphor" of identity whereby "to know who you are is to be orientated in moral space, a space in which questions arise about what is good or bad, what is worth doing and what not, what has meaning and importance for you and what is trivial and secondary." See Taylor, *Sources of the Self*, 28.

of the individualized self,[15] the social setting within which the New Testament was written prioritized collectivistic or group identity.[16] This raises the possibility that any tendency to over-individualize mission-commitment in contemporary discussion may be due, in part, to the cultural current in which *we* swim. This possibility is strengthened by the realization that central to Paul's mode of identity formation is the metaphor of temple—a missional identity that is fundamentally corporate in nature.

Identity formation refers to the way in which deep structures of thought are established and give rise to corresponding values and ethics.[17] Throughout 1 Corinthians, temple imagery serves as the primary way by which Paul orients ecclesial identity: vertically and horizontally. The community as temple belongs to God, having been built upon the foundation of the Messiah and inhabited by God's Spirit (3:11, 16). Moreover, this group identity places Paul's readers into a web of horizontal salvific relationships. Throughout 1 Cor 8:1—11:1, Corinthian self-understanding is reinforced by an appeal to their corporate identity as an alternative sacred community with obligations to seek the salvific welfare of others and to glorify God (10:23–33). Moreover, in 1 Cor 14:23-25, an explicit corporate missional identity reinforces the priority of prophecy through which the gentiles join the eschatological temple community. Like the body metaphor, which also assumes increasing prominence throughout the letter, ecclesial identity is essentially corporate. This is not to suggest that individual identity or mission-commitment is unimportant. Paul's point is that temple identity provides a moral framework in which individual salvific agency is outlined for the common good, whether it is marital commitment (7:12–16), temple dining (8:1–13) or one's choice of speech (14:1–25). To acknowledge that missional identity in 1 Corinthians is essentially corporate is not to downplay the importance of this

---

15. Taylor, *Sources of the Self*, 36.

16. Lim, *Metaphors and Social Identity*, §2.

17. Taylor refers to "inescapable frameworks" or "moral space" by which we make sense of our lives, on which see Taylor, *Sources of the Self*, 18, 28. See Tucker, *Reading 1 Corinthians*, §1–2.

individual agency, or even verbal modes of mission-commitment, but to broaden our contemporary missional imagination to recognize the myriad of ways in which horizontal salvific intentionality is to feature within, and through, the ecclesial community.

My intention throughout this book has been not only to observe missional expectations and identity formation but to "hear," along with the first readers, how Paul's writings may have nurtured the imagination, and compelled the actions, of the Corinthian community. Such collectivist notions of identity arguably play an important role for group cohesion, confidence, and effectiveness. This is especially true of a minority Christ-group in first-century Corinth whose small numbers—perhaps only 0.2 percent of the overall population—no doubt contributed to a fragile group identity. This may also explain why Paul seems more interested in forming a missional identity than outlining an explicit missionary commission. The establishment of deep structures of convictions may have been, from Paul's perspective, more necessary and effective over time in encouraging expressions of mission-commitment.

This observation of corporate missional identity may also serve the cohesion, confidence, and effectiveness of the contemporary church whose cultural standing in post-Christendom may increasingly be analogous to that of first-century Corinth. At the height of Christendom an emphasis on individualism and verbal modes of mission-commitment made sense. After all, Christendom provided a common ontological framework of understanding and a myriad of opportunities by which Christians could effectively speak to, and within, their culture. However, such platforms and a shared framework of understanding can no longer be assumed. Charles Taylor, tracing the rise of secularization in the modern West, points out that ours is the first civilization in which human flourishing is assumed to correspond to no transcendent reality outside of the self.[18] The changes we observe in Western culture are no mere shifts in cultural practices but a radical and unprecedented overturning of Christian epistemology and ontology. The present and emerging cultural context

18. Taylor, *Secular Age*, §Intro.4. See Taylor, *Sources of the Self*, 36.

in which we live in the West may need to increasingly draw deeply from the corporate missional identity that Paul cultivated in those early Corinthian Christians. Verbal modes of mission expression may need to be preceded, and complemented, by a comprehensive expression of our collective missional identity. This is not to suggest that individual and corporate expressions of mission are mutually exclusive, but conversion may increasingly need to be understood as a long process of engagement not just between individuals but between an unbeliever and a wider Christian community. These observations of missional identity in 1 Corinthians anticipate aspects of three further topics of relevance for contemporary church practice, namely, ecclesial boundaries, salvific agency, and the comprehensive nature of mission-commitment.

Soft Difference in Ecclesial Boundaries

The essentially corporate nature of the early Christian movement gives rise to the existence of insider and outsider identities, with a necessary boundary between the two groups. The identity of these two groups, and further groups inside each group, and the porous boundaries within the Corinthian church is, I believe, the most significant aspect of this study for contemporary missional practice. My claim stands in contrast to an enduring ecclesial tradition that seeks to uphold the internal purity of the church. Towards the end of the twentieth century, influential theologian Albert Mohler challenged the evangelical community, arguing that "the great task of the church is to prove itself to be the genuine church revealed in the New Testament—proving its authenticity by a demonstration of pure faith and authentic community."[19] This aim, according to Mohler, requires the recovery of the so-called "missing mark" of the church: *church discipline*.[20] It appears his call has been heeded—over the decades since he penned this charge, a growing body

19. Mohler, "Church Discipline," 186.
20. Mohler, "Church Discipline," 186.

of literature has appeared, both popular and for the academy, advancing the cause of disciplinary renewal in the church.[21] Central to the claims of this movement is the text of 1 Cor 5:1–8, which, it is argued, provides an example of the removal from membership of those who refuse to repent so that the purity and holiness of the church can be maintained.[22]

In chapter 1 of this book I challenged this simplistic reading of 1 Cor 5:1–8. I argued that a sociospiritual crisis formed the background of what was a rare apostolic decision to exclude someone from the community. Such a reading not only accounts for the literary context of this passage but also explains why Paul does not exclude those involved in similar incidents of impurity throughout the rest of the letter, even within the section immediately afterwards that also deals with sexual immorality (1 Cor 6–7). Indeed, central to the argument of this book has been the recognition that the Christian community in Corinth is untidy: Some insiders need to enter into a more authentic Christian identity (5:1–8). On the other hand, some outsiders are sufficiently socially connected that they are within the gathered community and then come to recognize the presence of God in ways that some insiders have yet to do (14:20–25). As one of the Anglican Articles of Faith states, "in the visible Church the evil be ever mingled with the good."[23] I am not suggesting that there is no place for what is referred to as church discipline, but I am proposing that Paul imagines the community in Corinth not simply as a place of purity but one of "spiritual formation."[24]

Such an untidy ecclesial reality challenges contemporary expressions of church community. The intrinsic tendency of any

---

21. For an accessible example, see Leeman, *Church and the Surprising Offense.* For a more technical biblio-theological monograph, see Bargerhuff, *Love That Rescues.*

22. Schreiner, "Biblical Basis," §5.

23. *Thirty-Nine Articles of Religion*, art. XXVI.

24. Hays, *Moral Vision*, 401–2.

group is towards self-preservation.[25] This being so, Miroslav Volf warns against forging identity through a "negative process":

> When identity is forged primarily through the negative process of the rejection of the beliefs and practices of others . . . we have to push others away from ourselves and keep them at a distance, and we have to close ourselves off from others to keep ourselves pure of their taint.[26]

Those who lament the missing mark of the church and call for a renewal of the principle of excommunication on the basis of 1 Cor 5:1–8 risk not only misapplying the text but also failing to contend with the missional potential of an untidy church community.

Throughout 1 Corinthians high levels of social integration with unbelievers, even at Christian gatherings, are not simply assumed but serve a vital means through which the believing community expresses its missional identity. Such an observation echoes Volf's "soft difference," a missional posture born not from fear or withdrawal but from a secure identity in God that enables "others space to be themselves" and where "mission fundamentally takes the form of witness and invitation."[27] This situation in Corinth may increasingly be analogous to the one in which the contemporary church finds itself. Post-Christendom may mean that churches need to creatively shape their community, providing different types and intensities of socioreligious gatherings that correspond more appropriately to the variety of gatherings, and porous boundaries, evident throughout 1 Corinthians. If the community is a means by which unbelievers may observe, be attracted to, and even themselves come to assume a Christian identity, then the gatherings of the church must, at least in some cases, become places to which Christians will want to invite their unbelieving family and friends.[28] "In a socially open community," René Breuel warns, "borders are translucent: there are people with different

---

25. Breuel, "Open Networks" in "Today's Social Path to Faith."
26. Volf, "Soft Difference," 21.
27. Volf, "Soft Difference," 24.
28. Keller, *Center Church*, 303–4.

degrees of spiritual maturity . . . . This brings a high level of diversity and ambiguity, which only a very mature leadership can manage."[29] Such maturity is what Paul invites the Corinthians, and us with them, to aspire to. And such aspirations belong not only to those in leadership but to the entire community of believers who have, in Paul's vision, the responsibility to serve the salvific welfare of outsiders as well as insiders.

Salvific Agency

A further application of 1 Corinthians missiology to contemporary practice arises from the way in which horizontal salvation language functions in 1 Corinthians to give agency to believers in a range of household, social, and ecclesial contexts. Such is remarkable when considered against the stratified context of Roman society in which those of higher social status held more influence than those of lower position. Indeed, differentiated social status is one of the significant issues that Paul addresses throughout 1 Corinthians. He does so by outlining a countercultural emphasis on the salvific responsibility and potential of the whole *body*. So, the gathered church exercises moral formation by protesting against a person of high social standing (1 Cor 5:1–8); wives are mentioned first as those conveying sanctifying influence towards their husbands (7:14); Paul identifies with the "Weak" so that such people would be saved (9:22); and all are part of the one body and drink of the same Spirit who distributes gifts to all (12:4–13). Even Paul and Apollos are "only servants, through whom you came to believe" (3:5). The salvific ministry of the Messiah belongs to the entire Corinthian ecclesial community (11:1).

Such democratization of salvific agency is an important insight for the contemporary church whose structures, according to Newbigin, too often reflect the static assumptions of Christendom. Michael Goheen summarizes the changing culture in which Newbigin found himself:

29. Breuel, "Translucent Borders" in "Today's Social Path to Faith."

> Not only was the church's place in society changing, but
> so was Western society itself . . . Christendom structures
> assumed a social organization in which the family, politi-
> cal, economic, and social life were intertwined in an in-
> divisible whole. The church located geographically in the
> center of that religio-political unity could perhaps stand
> as a sign of good news for the whole community. But by
> Newbigin's day, society was much more differentiated,
> complex, and mobile. A person lives in many "places" at
> the same time. The church needed new structures to be,
> do, and speak good news in this new social setting.[30]

To meet this new social setting in which the church finds itself
in the West, Newbigin proposes ecclesial structures that can pen-
etrate the various layers of neighborhood, work, sectors ("frontier-
groups"), and sociopolitical life.[31] His proposals, while general,
reflect his belief that "the whole life of the Church thus has a *missionary dimension.*"[32]

Behind such structural concerns lies an additional theological driver of missional stasis: the order of the church. Both Catholic
and Reformed traditions have left, in different ways, an enduring
legacy that draws an essential distinction between the ministry of
the ordained and that of the laity. In a penetrating analysis of the
evolution of the ordained ministry, David Bosch observes that every denomination has tended to enshrine a clergyman-priest into
a privileged position, serving as the linchpin of the church.[33] As an
ordained Anglican priest myself, I gladly affirm the representative
nature of ordained ministry while also lamenting where my tradition has underdeveloped the representative nature of *every* expression of ministry within the church. If contemporary ecclesial
structures are going to flex into the differentiated layers of modern
society, a deep theological commitment to the salvific agency of
every believer is required. The truth is, as Volf points out, "different

30. Goheen, *Church and Its Vocation*, 122.

31. Newbigin, *Gospel in a Pluralist Society*, 230–31. See Goheen, *Church and Its Vocation*, 124–26.

32. Newbigin, *One Body*, 21.

33. Bosch, *Transforming Mission*, 467–70.

persons can become the soteriologically 'significant others' for other persons."[34]

Mission as "Being"

In this final subsection in which I am applying the missiological principles of 1 Corinthians, I outline more fully what was anticipated in my earlier description of a corporate missional identity. That is, the fundamentally corporate nature of the temple image, along with the consistent usage of horizontal salvific language throughout the epistle, expresses an integrated and comprehensive embodiment of ecclesial mission-commitment.

One of the pitfalls, previously discussed, that results from limiting a missional investigation to Paul's theology and practice alone is the subsequent tendency to conceptually distinguish between passive and active expressions of mission.[35] Verbal proclamation, then, becomes most readily identified with *true* mission activity— after all, is not active better than passive? Yet, such a description of mission risks being an ideal rather than a lived experience—it narrows rather than broadens the missional imagination. It risks reducing the missional expression of the church to proclamation alone, whereas Paul is committed to this expansive summary: "So whether you eat or drink or whatever you do, do it for the glory of God. Do not cause anyone to stumble . . . I am not seeking my own good but the good of many, so that they may be saved. Follow my example" (1 Cor 10:31—11:1). This comprehensive description of mission-commitment most immediately summarizes the applied principles of integration and resistance regarding association with idol-food in the wider literary unit (8:1—11:1). An example from a prior section of 1 Corinthians that also demonstrates an embodied expression of mission is the description of salvific intent that is to characterize mixed marriages (7:12–16). In both cases, I borrowed the term *ethical apologetic* from Dickson to describe the way in

---

34. Volf, *After Our Likeness*, 226.

35. Bowers, "Church and Mission in Paul," 106.

which one's behavior is intended to attract outsiders. By adopting a method from below that accounts for the missional expectations which Paul lays upon his readers, including the way in which he forms their missional identity, this book has offered an account of ecclesial missiology that integrates verbal and behavioral modes of mission-commitment.

This embodied description corresponds to Bosch's account of mission as a matter of "being" rather than doing.[36] He writes, "Evangelism is only possible when the community that evangelizes—the church—is a radiant manifestation of the Christian faith and exhibits an attractive lifestyle."[37] This is not to suggest that the church will be liked nor even tolerated. We are not, as Newbigin points out, returning to the past—to a Constantinian authority nor a pre-Constantinian innocence.[38] Rather we hold to the "impossible possibility" of salvation[39]—avoiding a default Pelagian reliance on ourselves, we look to the one whose salvific act in the world was Christ crucified: "a stumbling block to Jews and foolishness to gentiles . . . For the foolishness of God is wiser than human wisdom, and the weakness of God is stronger than human strength" (1 Cor 1:23, 25). Given this, the only way for the gospel to be credible is through what Newbigin calls the congregation as "hermeneutic of the gospel":

> The only hermeneutic of the gospel is a congregation of men and women who believe it and live by it. I am, of course, not denying the importance of the many activities by which we seek to challenge public life with the gospel—evangelistic campaigns, distributions of Bibles and Christian literature, conferences and even books such as this one. But I am saying that these are all secondary, and that they have power to accomplish

36. Bosch, "Hermeneutical Principles," 34.

37. Bosch, *Transforming Mission*, 414.

38. Newbigin, *Gospel in a Pluralist Society*, 223–24.

39. Newbigin, *Gospel in a Pluralist Society*, 224.

their purpose only as they are rooted and lead back to a believing community.[40]

In other words, the lived experience of the ecclesial community must both challenge and attract the society in which it exists, offering an alternative plausibility and belief structure by which unbelievers can begin to consider the claims of Christianity. Such unbelievers may need to belong before they believe, proceeding through a series of "mini-decisions" before they experience genuine conversion.[41] The vertical salvific Christ event, with which this book began, cannot exist separately from the community that is being saved. That community itself carries the message of this event to those within their church and to those outside, as ethics and speech together are integrated and ordered for the salvific welfare of others. This book has explored only one of Paul's letters. Other scholarly contributions have noted further examples from the Pauline corpus, including financial assistance of "missionaries," praying for the conversion of others, and the salvific potential of public praise.[42] Such examples, together with those proposed throughout this book, are concrete expressions of the corporate missional identity into which Paul is forming his readers. Far from limiting mission-commitment to verbal modes of communication, these examples demonstrate that Paul intends to nurture and widen the missional imagination of his readers as they locate themselves in the *missio Dei*.

CONCLUSION

While Paul's first letter to the Corinthians is not typically associated with New Testament ecclesial missiological reflection, this study has demonstrated that it is indeed a rich resource for such. By approaching a theology of mission through salvific language

40. Newbigin, *Gospel in a Pluralist Society*, 227.

41. Keller, *Center Church*, 281–82.

42. Dickson, *Mission-Commitment*, 10. Note that Dickson offers some further distinctions within his two categories of a verbal and ethical apologetic.

and associated concepts, this study has outlined a series of Pauline expectations that provide an exegetical basis for a robust ecclesial missional identity. Casting the Corinthian church as the eschatological temple community, Paul emphasizes their vertical belonging to God as well as their participation in a series of horizontal relationships characterized by a concern for the salvific welfare of the church of God. Moreover, as those newly incorporated into this community, a salvific concern was also to extend to outside Jews and gentiles towards whom Paul cultivated a missional imagination in such circumstances as mixed marriages, the socioreligious environment of wider Corinth, and even within the Corinthians' own religious gatherings where such unbelievers were also present. Such an ecclesial picture cannot be accounted for by the mere conceptual category of a passive role in mission partnership. Paul fosters a sense of agency in his readers, that they might convey salvific good upon others, and this manifests itself through an integrated ethical and verbal expression of this salvific intentionality. By drawing from the tools of rhetorical analysis and sociohistorical inquiry, along with emerging social identity theories, this study has demonstrated that close literary analysis of the text itself has in fact yielded a rich ecclesial missiology in Paul's first letter to the Corinthians. By outlining the ways in which Paul expected his readers to adopt a posture of salvific intentionality in the complex social setting of mid-first-century Roman Corinth, an answer to the so-called riddle of ecclesial mission has emerged—the great omission has been demonstrated to be merely apparent, as an explicitly exegetical voice, grounded in 1 Corinthians, has been added to the emerging conversation of missional hermeneutics.

Bibliography

Aland, Barbara, et al., eds. *The Greek New Testament*. 5th revised ed. Stuttgart: Deutsche Bibelgesellschaft, 2014.

Bailey, Kenneth E. *Paul through Mediterranean Eyes: Cultural Studies in 1 Corinthians*. Downers Grove: IVP Academic, 2011.

Bargerhuff, Eric J. *Love That Rescues: God's Fatherly Love in the Practice of Church Discipline*. Eugene, OR: Wipf & Stock, 2010.

Barnett, Paul W. *The Corinthian Question: Why Did the Church Oppose Paul?* Nottingham: Apollos, 2011.

———. *Jerusalem to Illyricum: Earliest Christianity through the Eyes of Paul*. Eugene, OR: Cascade, 2022. Kindle ed.

Barram, Michael. *Mission and Moral Reflection in Paul*. SBL 75. New York: Peter Lang, 2006.

———. "Pauline Mission as Salvific Intentionality: Fostering a Missional Consciousness in 1 Corinthians 9:19–23 and 10:31—11.1." In *Paul as Missionary: Identity, Theology, and Practice*, edited by Trevor J. Burke and Brian S. Rosner, 324–46. LNTS 420. London: T. & T. Clark, 2011.

Barton, Stephen C. "Sanctification and Oneness in 1 Corinthians with Implications for the Case of 'Mixed Marriages' (1 Corinthians 7:12–16)." *NTS* 63 (2017) 38–55.

Bauer, Walter, et al. *A Greek-English Lexicon of the New Testament and Other Early Christian Literature*. 3rd ed. Chicago: University of Chicago Press, 2000.

Beale, G. K. *The Temple and the Church's Mission: A Biblical Theology of the Dwelling Place of God*. NSBT 17. Leicester: Apollos, 2004.

Bender, Kimlyn J. *1 Corinthians*. Brazos Theological Commentary on the Bible. Grand Rapids: Brazos, 2022. Kindle ed.

Bookidis, Nancy. "Religion in Corinth: 146 B.C.E. to 100 C.E." In *Urban Religion in Roman Corinth: Interdisciplinary Approaches*, edited by Daniel N. Schowalter and Steven J. Friesen, 141–64. Harvard Theological Series 53. Cambridge, MA: Harvard University Press, 2005.

———. "Ritual Dining at Corinth." In *Greek Sanctuaries: New Approaches*, edited by Nanno Marinatos and Robin Hägg, 45–61. Abingdon, UK: Routledge, 1993.

Bosch, David J. "Hermeneutical Principles in the Biblical Foundation for Mission." *Evangelical Review of Theology* 17.4 (1993) 24–35.

———. "Mission in Biblical Perspective." *International Review of Mission* 74.296 (1985) 531–38.

———. *Transforming Mission: Paradigm Shifts in Theology of Mission*. American Society of Missiology Series 16. Maryknoll, NY: Orbis, 1991.

Bowers, Paul. "Church and Mission in Paul." *JSNT* 44 (1991) 89–111.

Breuel, René. "Today's Social Path to Faith." https://redeemercitytocity.com/articles-stories/todays-social-path-to-faith.

Brock, Brian, and Bernd Wannenwetsch. *The Malady of the Christian Body*. Vol. 1 of *A Theological Exposition of Paul's First Letter to the Corinthians*. Eugene, OR: Cascade, 2016. Kindle ed.

Buell, Denise Kimber. *Why This New Race: Ethnic Reasoning in Early Christianity*. New York: Columbia University Press, 2005.

Campbell, Constantine R. *Verbal Aspect and Non-Indicative Verbs: Further Soundings in the Greek of the New Testament*. Studies in Biblical Greek 13. New York: Peter Lang, 2009.

Carson, D. A. *Showing the Spirit: A Theological Exposition of 1 Corinthians 12–14*. Moore Theological College Lecture Series. Homebush West, NSW: Lancer, 1988.

Chambers, Stephen Lionel. "Paul, His Converts, and Mission in First Corinthians." PhD diss., University of St. Michael's College, 2004.

Chester, Stephen J. "Divine Madness? Speaking in Tongues in 1 Corinthians 14:23." *JSNT* 27.4 (2005) 417–46.

Cheung, Alex T. *Idol Food in Corinth: Jewish Background and Pauline Legacy*. JSNTSup 176. Sheffield: Sheffield Academic Press, 1999.

Chow, John K. *Patronage and Power: A Study of Social Networks in Corinth*. JSNTSup 75. Sheffield: JSOT, 1992.

Chrysostom, John. "Homilies on the Epistle of Paul to the Corinthians 4.4." In *1–2 Corinthians*, edited by Gerald Bray, 206–7. Ancient Christian Commentary on Scripture: New Testament 7. Downers Grove, IL: IVP 1999.

———. "Homilies on the Epistle of Paul to the Corinthians 15.5." In *1–2 Corinthians*, edited by Gerald Bray, 47. Ancient Christian Commentary on Scripture: New Testament 7. Downers Grove, IL: IVP, 1999.

———. "Homilies on the Epistle of Paul to the Corinthians 19.4." In *1–2 Corinthians*, edited by Gerald Bray, 64. Ancient Christian Commentary on Scripture: New Testament 7. Downers Grove, IL: IVP, 1999.

———. "Homilies on the Epistle of Paul to the Corinthians 36.2." In *1–2 Corinthians*, edited by Gerald Bray, 142. Ancient Christian Commentary on Scripture: New Testament 7. Downers Grove, IL: IVP, 1999.

Ciampa, Roy E. "Prophecy in Corinth and Paul's Use of Isaiah's Prophecy in 1 Corinthians 14:21–25." In *Scripture, Texts, and Tracings in 1 Corinthians*, edited by Linda L. Belleville and B. J. Oropeza, 141–59. Lanham, MD: Lexington, 2019.

Ciampa, Roy, and Brain S. Rosner. *The First Letter to the Corinthians.* The Pillar New Testament Commentary. Grand Rapids: Eerdmans, 2010.

Clarke, Andrew D. "Church Membership and the ἰδιώτης in the Early Corinthian Community." In *New Testament Theology in Light of the Church's Mission: Essays in Honor of I. Howard Marshall*, edited by Jon C. Laansma et al., 197–211. Eugene, OR: Cascade, 2011.

Cohick, Lynn H. *The Letter to the Ephesians.* NICNT. Grand Rapids: Eerdmans, 2020. Kindle ed.

———. *Women in the World of the Earliest Christians: Illuminating Ancient Ways of Life.* Grand Rapids: Baker Academic, 2009. Kindle ed.

Collins, Raymond F. *First Corinthians.* Sacra Pagina. Collegeville, MN: Liturgical, 1999.

Conzelmann, Hans. *1 Corinthians: A Commentary on the First Epistle to the Corinthians.* Translated by George W. MacRae. Hermeneia: A Critical and Historical Commentary on the Bible. Philadelphia: Fortress, 1975.

deSilva, David A. *Honor, Patronage, Kinship and Purity: Unlocking the New Testament Culture.* Downers Grove, IL: IVP, 2000.

Dickson, John P. "Gospel as News: εὐαγγελ- from Aristophanes to the Apostle Paul." *NTS* 51 (2005) 212–30.

———. *Mission-Commitment in Ancient Judaism and in the Pauline Communities: The Shape, Extent and Background of Early Christian Mission.* WUNT 2.159. Tübingen: Mohr Siebeck, 2003.

Ellington, Dustin W. "Imitating Paul's Relationship to the Gospel: 1 Corinthians 8:1—11:1." *JSNT* 33.3 (2011) 303–15.

Fee, Gordon D. "εἰδωλόθυτα Once Again: An Interpretation of 1 Corinthians 8–10." *Biblica* 61 (1980) 127–97.

———. *The First Epistle to the Corinthians.* NICNT. Grand Rapids: Eerdmans, 1987.

Fitzmyer, Joseph A. *First Corinthians: A New Translation with Introduction and Commentary.* The Anchor Yale Bible 32. New Haven, CT: Yale University Press, 2008.

Fotopoulos, John. "Arguments Concerning Food Offered to Idols: Corinthian Quotations and Pauline Refutations in a Rhetorical Partitio (1 Corinthians 8:1–9)." *CBQ* 67 (2005) 611–31.

Frost, Michael. *Exiles: Living Missionally in a Post-Christian Culture.* Peabody, MA: Hendrickson, 2006.

Garland, David E. *1 Corinthians.* Baker Exegetical Commentary of the New Testament. Grand Rapids: Baker Academic, 2003.

Gillihan, Yonder Moynihan. "Jewish Laws on Illicit Marriage, the Defilement of Offspring, and the Holiness of the Temple: A New Halakic Interpretation of 1 Corinthians 7:14." *JBL* 121.4 (2002) 711–44.

Goheen, Michael W. *The Church and Its Vocation: Lesslie Newbigin's Missionary Ecclesiology*. Grand Rapids: Baker Academic, 2018.

Gooch, Peter D. *Dangerous Food: 1 Corinthians 8–10 in Its Context*. Studies in Christianity and Judaism 5. Waterloo, ON: Wilfrid Laurier University Press, 1993.

Gorman, Michael. *Becoming the Gospel: Paul, Participation, and Mission*. Grand Rapids: Eerdmans, 2015. Kindle ed.

———. "First Corinthians and the Marks of God's *Ekklēsia*: One, Holy, Catholic and Apostolic." In *One God, One People, One Future: Essays in Honour of N. T. Wright*, edited by John Anthony Dunne and Eric Lewellen, 136–54. London: SPCK, 2018.

Green, Michael. *Evangelism in the Early Church*. Grand Rapids: Eerdmans, 1970.

Gundry Volf, Judith M. *Paul and Perseverance: Staying In and Falling Away*. WUNT 2.37. Tübingen: Mohr, 1990.

Guthrie, George H. *2 Corinthians*. Baker Exegetical Commentary on the New Testament. Grand Rapids: Baker Academic, 2015.

Hall, David R. *The Unity of the Corinthian Correspondence*. JSNTSup 251. London: T. & T. Clark, 2003.

Hays, Richard B. *First Corinthians*. Interpretation. Louisville, KY: John Knox, 1997. Kindle ed.

———. *The Moral Vision of the New Testament: A Contemporary Introduction to New Testament Ethics*. New York: T. & T. Clark, 1996.

Heil, John Paul. *The Rhetorical Role of Scripture in 1 Corinthians*. SBL 15. Atlanta: Society of Biblical Literature, 2005.

Hill, Michael. *The How and Why of Love: An Introduction to Evangelical Ethics*. Kingsford, NSW: Matthias Media, 2002.

Hodge, Caroline Johnson. "Married to an Unbeliever: Households, Hierarchies, and Holiness in 1 Corinthians 7:12–16." *HTR* 103.1 (2010) 1–25.

Hodge, Charles. *A Commentary on 1 & 2 Corinthians*. 1 vol. ed. The Geneva Series of Commentaries. Edinburgh: Banner of Truth, 1974.

Horrell, David G. "Fear, Hope, and Doing Good: Wives as a Paradigm of Mission in 1 Peter." *Estudios Bílicos* 73.3 (2015) 409–29.

———. *The Making of Christian Morality: Reading Paul in Ancient and Modern Contexts*. Grand Rapids: Eerdmans, 2019.

———. *Solidarity and Difference: A Contemporary Reading of Paul's Ethics*. London: T. & T. Clark, 2005.

Hunsberger, George R. "Proposals for a Missional Hermeneutic: Mapping a Conversation." *Missiology: An International Review* 34.4 (2001) 309–21.

Hurtado, Larry W. *Destroyer of the gods: Early Christian Distinctiveness in the Roman World*. Waco: Baylor University Press, 2016.

Instone-Brewer, David. *Divorce and Remarriage in the Bible: The Social and Literary Context*. Grand Rapids: Eerdmans, 2002. Kindle ed.

Jeremias, Joachim. "Die missionarische Aufgabe in der Mischehe (I Kor. 7, 16)." In *Neutestamentliche Studien für Rudolf Bultmann*, 255–60. 2nd rev. ed. BZNW 21. Berlin: Alfred Töpelmann, 1957.

Johanson, B. C. "Tongues, a Sign for Unbelievers? A Structural and Exegetical Study of 1 Corinthians 14:20–25." *NTS* 25 (1978–79) 180–203.

Josephus. *Against Apion*. Translated by William Whiston. 1 vol. Peabody, MA: Hendrickson, 1987.

———. *Jewish Antiquities*. Translated by William Whiston. 1 vol. Peabody, MA: Hendrickson, 1987.

———. *The Jewish War*. Translated by William Whiston. 1 vol. Peabody, MA: Hendrickson, 1987.

Judge, E. A. "The Social Pattern of Christian Groups in the First Century." In *Social Distinctives of the Christians in the First Century: Pivotal Essays by E. A. Judge*, edited by David M. Scholer. Grand Rapids: Baker Academic, 2008. Kindle ed.

Keller, Timothy. *Center Church: Doing Balanced, Gospel-Centered Ministry in Your City*. Grand Rapids: Zondervan, 2012.

Kistemaker, Simon. "Deliver This Man to Satan (1 Cor. 5:5): Case Study in Church Discipline." *Master's Seminary Journal* 3 (1992) 33–45.

———. *Exposition of the First Epistle to the Corinthians*. New Testament Commentary. Grand Rapids: Baker, 1993.

Kloppenborg, John S. *Christ's Associations: Connecting and Belonging in the Ancient City*. New Haven, CT: Yale University Press, 2019.

Köstenberger, Andreas J., and Peter T. O'Brien. *Salvation to the Ends of the Earth: A Biblical Theology of Mission*. NSBT 11. Downers Grove, IL: IVP, 2001.

Kubo, Sakae. "1 Corinthians 7:16: Optimistic or Pessimistic?" *NTS* 24.4 (1978) 539–44.

Lang, T. J. "Trouble with Insiders: The Social Profile of the ἄπιστοι in Paul's Corinthian Correspondence." *JBL* 137.4 (2018) 981–1001.

Lee-Barnewell, Michelle. "Turning Κεφαλή on Its Head: The Rhetoric of Reversal in Ephesians 5:21–33." In *Christian Origins and Greco-Roman Culture: Social and Literary Contexts for the New Testament*, edited by Stanley E. Porter and Andrew W. Pitts, 599–614. Vol. 1 of *Early Christianity in Its Hellenistic Context*. Texts and Editions for New Testament Study 9. Leiden: Brill, 2013.

Leeman, Jonathan. *The Church and the Surprising Offense of God's Love: Reintroducing the Doctrines of Church Membership and Discipline*. Wheaton: Crossway, 2010.

Lim, Kar Long. *Metaphors and Social Identity Formation in Paul's Letters to the Corinthians*. Eugene, OR: Pickwick, 2017. Kindle ed.

López, René A. "Does the Vice List in 1 Corinthians 6:9–10 Describe Believers or Unbelievers." *Bibliotheca Sacra* 164 (2017) 59–73.

Malcolm, Matthew R. *The World of 1 Corinthians: An Exegetical Source Book of Literary and Visual Background*. Milton Keynes: Paternoster, 2012.

Martin, Dale B. *The Corinthian Body*. New Haven, CT: Yale University Press, 1995.

Martin, Ralph. *Worship in the Early Church*. 3rd ed. Grand Rapids: Eerdmans, 1974.

McKinzie, Greg. "Missional Hermeneutics as Theological Interpretation." *JTI* 11.2 (2017) 157–79.

McKnight, Scot. *A Light among the Gentiles: Jewish Missionary Activity in the Second Temple Period*. Minneapolis: Fortress, 1991.

McNamara, Derek. "Shame the Incestuous Man: 1 Corinthians 5." *Neotestamentica* 44.2 (2010) 307–26.

Meeks, Wayne A. *The First Urban Christians: The Social World of the Apostle Paul*. New Haven, CT: Yale University Press, 1983.

———. "A Hermeneutics of Social Embodiment." In *Search of the Early Christians: Selected Essays*, edited by Allen R. Hilton and H. Gregor Snyder, 185–95. New Haven, CT: Yale University Press, 2002.

Moberly, R. W. L. *Prophecy and Discernment*. Cambridge, UK: Cambridge University Press, 2006.

Mohler, Albert R. Jr. "Church Discipline: The Missing Mark." In *The Compromised Church: The Present Evangelical Crisis*, edited by John H. Armstrong, 171–88. Wheaton: Crossway, 1998.

Morris, Leon. "Salvation." In *Dictionary of Paul and His Letters*, edited by Gerald F. Hawthorne and Ralph P. Martin, 858–62. Downers Grove, IL: IVP, 1993.

Motyer, Alec. *The Prophecy of Isaiah*. Leicester, England: IVP, 1993.

Munoz, Kevin A. "How Not to Go out of the World: First Corinthians 14:13–25 and the Social Foundations of Early Christian Expansion." PhD diss., Graduate School of Emory University, 2008.

Murphy-O'Connor, Jerome. *Keys to First Corinthians: Revisiting the Major Issues*. Oxford: Oxford University Press, 2009.

———. *St. Paul's Corinth: Texts and Archeology*. 3rd ed. Collegeville, MN: Liturgical, 2002.

Nash, Robert Scott. *1 Corinthians*. Smyth & Helwys Bible Commentary. Macon, GA: Smyth & Helwys, 2009.

Newbigin, Lesslie. "England as a Foreign Mission Field." https://newbigin resources.org/1986-england-as-a-foreign-mission-field/.

———. *Foolishness to the Greeks: The Gospel and Western Culture*. London: SPCK, 1986.

———. *The Gospel in a Pluralist Society*. Grand Rapids: Eerdmans, 1989.

———. *One Body, One Gospel, One World: The Christian Mission Today*. New York: International Missionary Council, 1958.

Nissen, Johannes. *New Testament and Mission: Historical and Hermeneutical Perspectives*. Frankfurt: Peter Lang, 1995.

O'Brien, Peter T. *Consumed by Passion: Paul and the Dynamic of the Gospel*. Homebush West, NSW: Lancer, 1993.

O'Donovan, Oliver. *Resurrection and Moral Order: An Outline of Evangelical Ethics*. 2nd ed. Leicester, England: Apollos, 1994.

———. *Self, World, and Time*. Ethics as Theology 1. Grand Rapids: Eerdmans, 2013.

Peppiatt, Lucy. *Women and Worship at Corinth: Paul's Rhetorical Arguments in 1 Corinthians*. Eugene, OR: Cascade, 2015. Kindle ed.

Perkins, Pheme. *First Corinthians*. ΠΑΙΔΕΙΑ Paideia: Commentaries on the New Testament. Grand Rapids: Baker Academic, 2012.

Philo. *The Special Laws*. Translated by F. H. Colson et al. 11 vols. LCL. Cambridge, MA: Harvard University Press, 1929–62.

Plummer, Robert. *Paul's Understanding of the Church's Mission: Did the Apostle Paul Expect the Early Christian Communities to Evangelize?* Paternoster Biblical Monographs. Milton Keynes, UK: Paternoster, 2006.

Plutarch. "Advice to the Bride and Groom." In *Plutarch's Advice to the Bride and Groom and a Consolation to His Wife: English Translations, Commentary, Interpretive Essays, and Bibliography*, translated by Donald Russell, edited by Sarah B. Pomeroy, 5–14. New York: Oxford University Press, 1999.

Pratt, Zane, et al. *Introduction to Global Mission*. Nashville: B&H, 2014.

Rahlfs, Alfred, ed. *Septuaginta*. Stuttgart: Deutsche Bibelgesellschaft, 1935.

Reno, Joshua M. "Struggling Sages: Pauline Rhetoric and Social Control." *CBQ* 80.3 (2018) 827–47.

Rice, Joshua. *Paul and Patronage: The Dynamics of Power in 1 Corinthians*. Eugene, OR: Pickwick, 2013.

Robertson, O. Palmer. "Tongues: Sign of Covenantal Curse and Blessing." *Westminster Theological Journal* 38 (1975) 43–53.

Rosner, Brian S. "The Glory of God in Paul's Missionary Theology and Practice." In *Paul as Missionary: Identity, Activity, Theology, and Practice*, edited by Trevor J. Burke and Brian S. Rosner, 158–68. LNTS 420. London: T. & T. Clark International, 2011.

———. "The Missionary Character of 1 Corinthians." In *New Testament Theology in Light of the Church's Mission: Essays in Honor of I. Howard Marshall*, edited by Jon C. Laansma et al., 181–96. Eugene, OR: Cascade, 2011.

———. "Temple and Holiness in 1 Corinthians 5." *TynBul* 42.1 (1991) 137–45.

Sallares, J. Robert. "Meals." In *The Oxford Classical Dictionary*, edited by Simon Hornblower et al., 916. 4th ed. Oxford: Oxford University Press, 2012.

Schreiner, Thomas R. "The Biblical Basis for Church Discipline." In *Those Who Must Give an Account: A Study of Church Membership and Church Discipline*, edited by John S. Hammett and Benjamin L. Merkle, §5. Nashville: B & H Academic, 2012. Kindle ed.

Schütz, John Howard. *Paul and the Anatomy of Apostolic Authority*. 2nd ed. Louisville: Westminster John Knox, 2007.

Smith, Dennis E. *From Symposium to Eucharist: The Banquet in the Early Christian World*. Minneapolis: Fortress, 2003. Kindle ed.

Still, E. Coye III. "Paul's Aims Regarding εἰδωλόθυτα: A New Proposal for Interpreting 1 Corinthians 8:1—11:1." *Novum Testamentum* 44.4 (2002) 333–43.

Suh, Michael K. W. *Power and Peril: Paul's Use of Temple Discourse in 1 Corinthians*. BZNW 239. Berlin: de Gruyter, 2020. Kindle ed.

Taylor, Charles. *A Secular Age*. Cambridge, MA: Harvard University Press, 2007. Kindle ed.

———. *Sources of the Self: The Making of the Modern Identity*. Cambridge, MA: Harvard University Press, 1989.

Temple, William. "The Church." In *Oxford Dictionary of Quotations*, edited by Elizabeth Knowles, 766. 8th ed. Oxford: Oxford University Press, 2014.

Theissen, Gerd. "Social Conflicts in the Corinthian Community: Further Remarks on J. J. Meggitt, Paul, Poverty and Survival." *JSNT* 25.3 (2003) 371–91.

———. *The Social Setting of Pauline Christianity: Essays on Corinth*. Edited and translated by John H. Schütz. Philadelphia: Fortress, 1982.

The Thirty-Nine Articles of Religion. http://anglicansonline.org/basics/thirty-nine_articles.html.

Thiselton, Anthony C. *The First Epistle to the Corinthians: A Commentary on the Greek Text*. NIGTC. Grand Rapids: Eerdmans, 2000.

Tite, Philip L. "Roman Diet and Meat Consumption: Reassessing Elite Access to Meat in 1 Corinthians 8 and 10." *JSNT* 42.2 (2019) 185–222.

Tomson, Peter J. *Paul and the Jewish Law: Halakha in the Letters of the Apostle to the Gentiles*. Vol. 1 of *Jewish Traditions in Early Christian Literature*. Compendia Rerum Iudaicarum ad Novum Testamentum 3. Assen, Netherlands: Van Gorcum, 1990.

Treggiari, Susan. "Marriage and Family in Roman Society." In *Marriage and Family in the Biblical World*, edited by Ken M. Campbell, 132–82. Downers Grove, IL: IVP, 2003.

Tucker, Brian. "1 Corinthians." In *T. & T. Clark Social Identity Commentary on the New Testament*, edited by J. Brian Tucker and Aaron Kuecker, 293–326. London: T. & T. Clark, 2018.

———. *Reading 1 Corinthians*. Eugene, OR: Cascade, 2017. Kindle ed.

———. "The Role of Civic Identity on the Pauline Mission in Corinth." Διδασκαλία 19.1 (2008) 71–91.

van Aarde, Timothy A., and Lygunda li-M. "A Fruitful Missional Exegesis for a Missional Hermeneutic and Missiology." *In die Skriflig* 51.2 (2017) 1–10. https://doi.org/10.4102/ids.v51i2.2235.

Volf, Miroslav. *After Our Likeness: The Church as the Image of the Trinity*. Grand Rapids: Eerdmans, 1998.

———. "Soft Difference: Theological Reflections on the Relation between Church and Culture in 1 Peter." *Ex Auditu* 10 (1994) 15–30.

Ware, James. "The Thessalonians as a Missionary Congregation: 1 Thessalonians 1:5–8." *ZNTW* 83 (1992) 126–31.

Webb, Barry. *The Message of Isaiah: On Eagle's Wings*. BST. Leicester, England: IVP, 1996.

Westfall, Cynthia Long. "'This Is a Great Metaphor!' Reciprocity in the Ephesians Household Code." In *Christian Origins and Greco-Roman Culture: Social and Literary Contexts for the New Testament*, edited by Stanley E. Porter and Andrew W. Pitts, 561–98. Vol. 1 of *Early Christianity in Its Hellenistic Context*. Texts and Editions for New Testament Study 9. Leiden: Brill, 2013.

Willet, Rinse. "Whirlwind of Numbers—Demographic Experiment for Roman Corinth." *Ancient Society* 42 (2012) 127–58.

Willis, Wendell Lee. "Paul's Instructions to the Corinthian Church on the Eating of Idol Meat." PhD diss., Southern Methodist University, 1981.

Winter, Bruce W. *After Paul Left Corinth: The Influence of Secular Ethics and Social Change.* Grand Rapids: Eerdmans, 2001. Kindle ed.

Witherington, Ben III. *Conflict and Community in Corinth: A Socio-Rhetorical Commentary on 1 and 2 Corinthians.* Grand Rapids: Eerdmans, 1995.

Works, Carla Swafford. *The Church in the Wilderness: Paul's Use of Exodus Traditions in 1 Corinthians.* WUNT 2. Reihe 379. Tübingen: Mohr Siebeck, 2014.

Wright, Christopher J. H. *The Mission of God: Unlocking the Bible's Grand Narrative.* Downers Grove, IL: IVP, 2006.

Wright, N. T. *The Climax of the Covenant: Christ and the Law in Pauline Theology.* Minneapolis: Fortress, 1994.

———. *The Resurrection of the Son of God.* Vol. 3 of *Christian Origins and the Question of God.* Minneapolis: Fortress, 2003.

Index of Authors

Index of Subjects